Business Guides on the Go

"Business Guides on the Go" presents cutting-edge insights from practice on particular topics within the fields of business, management, and finance. Written by practitioners and experts in a concise and accessible form the series provides professionals with a general understanding and a first practical approach to latest developments in business strategy, leadership, operations, HR management, innovation and technology management, marketing or digitalization. Students of business administration or management will also benefit from these practical guides for their future occupation/careers.

These Guides suit the needs of today's fast reader.

More information about this series at
https://link.springer.com/bookseries/16836

Thomas Suwelack • Manuel Stegemann
Feng Xia Ang

Creating a Customer Experience-Centric Startup

A Step-by-Step Framework

Thomas Suwelack
Digital Customer Experience
Brand University of Applied Sciences
Hamburg, Germany

Manuel Stegemann
Consumer Psychology and Marketing
University of Applied Sciences
Bielefeld, Germany

Feng Xia Ang
21done Limited
Hamburg, Germany

ISSN 2731-4758 ISSN 2731-4766 (electronic)
Business Guides on the Go
ISBN 978-3-030-92457-7 ISBN 978-3-030-92458-4 (eBook)
https://doi.org/10.1007/978-3-030-92458-4

© The Editor(s) (if applicable) and The Author(s), under exclusive licence to Springer Nature Switzerland AG 2022

This work is subject to copyright. All rights are solely and exclusively licensed by the Publisher, whether the whole or part of the material is concerned, specifically the rights of translation, reprinting, reuse of illustrations, recitation, broadcasting, reproduction on microfilms or in any other physical way, and transmission or information storage and retrieval, electronic adaptation, computer software, or by similar or dissimilar methodology now known or hereafter developed.

The use of general descriptive names, registered names, trademarks, service marks, etc. in this publication does not imply, even in the absence of a specific statement, that such names are exempt from the relevant protective laws and regulations and therefore free for general use.

The publisher, the authors and the editors are safe to assume that the advice and information in this book are believed to be true and accurate at the date of publication. Neither the publisher nor the authors or the editors give a warranty, expressed or implied, with respect to the material contained herein or for any errors or omissions that may have been made. The publisher remains neutral with regard to jurisdictional claims in published maps and institutional affiliations.

This Springer imprint is published by the registered company Springer Nature Switzerland AG.
The registered company address is: Gewerbestrasse 11, 6330 Cham, Switzerland

Preface

Dear Reader,

We are happy that you are reading these lines and hope you continue to get a clear and practice-oriented overview on how to create a customer experience-centric start-up. In 2020, two of the three authors started the journey to create a start-up, 21done, that aims to "make personal growth and purpose a habit" on a wider scale in today's society. Independent of the result of this journey, we are already happy to have made this challenging experience.

While creating, innovating, and improvising on many ends is an enjoyable task, creating a new company is hard: First, it is hard from a mental perspective. Most founders think about their start-up 24/7. They wake up brainstorming the marketing strategy or thinking about a better revenue model. And go to bed contemplating a change in the team to become more productive. A founder struggles to remember the holiday plan of a friend and worries about the upcoming product feature launch even when out in a bar. Second, nine out of ten start-ups fail, resulting in not only financial loss for investors but also years of potentially wasted time investments of the founders.

Creating a new company *that excels in the market* is even harder. The ultimate key to this is to create excellent customer experiences, which requires the organisation to focus on this core company KPI in every part of the company and every day of work. Unfortunately, most companies do not follow this practice and therefore do not stand out in the wide landscape of businesses. We strongly believe that this is due to a lack of focus on the most important aspects to consider when operating a business as well as a lack of structured process on how to create excellent customer experiences on a daily basis.

This book is meant to support start-ups and founders (but also managers in bigger companies that aim to launch new product innovations) who invest a lot of energy, acting like an athlete, taking care of the interests of different stakeholders to increase chances to succeed in the market.

Hence, the following are the main contributions of this book:

- Provide a clear step-by-step framework to create a customer experience-centric company.
- Introduce the most impactful tools that managers can use to successfully complete every step of our framework.
- Guide managers through the process of creating a start-up, which is less about magically coming up with innovative business ideas, but rather about applying proven principles in a new context.

Overall, we aimed for a well-structured and easy-to-apply customer experience framework that defines customer experience as the start and end point of all business activities. The framework steps and tools (such as NPS, Empathy Map, Customer Journey, Golden Circle, Design Thinking, A/B-Testing) are designed to have a maximum impact on the customer experience, which is key to generate repeat buyers that become fans of the company. The toolbox contains tools from different disciplines, such as management, design, digitisation or psychology—as only an interdisciplinary approach enables superior insights for initiating the right customer activities in today's highly competitive times. If you are hesitant to read on, you may find the illustrated customer experience framework in Sect. 3.3 helpful.

We wish you a fruitful reading experience. If you have any questions or suggestions regarding the contents of the book, please do not hesitate to contact us.

Hamburg, Germany Thomas Suwelack
Bielefeld, Germany Manuel Stegemann
Hamburg, Germany Feng Xia Ang

Contents

1	**Introduction**	1
	References	3
2	**Concept, Relevance, and Management of CX**	5
	2.1 Concept of CX	5
	2.1.1 Definition	6
	2.1.2 Experience Types	6
	2.2 Relevance of CX	12
	2.2.1 The Experience Economy	12
	2.2.2 Customer Experience and Corporate Success	15
	2.3 Management of CX	17
	2.3.1 Understanding Touchpoints to Increase Customer Experience	20
	2.3.2 Context	22
	2.3.3 CX Measurement	24
	References	28
3	**Starting a Start-Up**	33
	3.1 The Founding Idea	33
	3.2 The Start-Up Pitch	35
	3.2.1 One-Sentence Pitch	37
	3.2.2 Pitch Deck	38

		3.3 Step-by-Step Framework to Create a CX-Centric Start-Up	49
		References	51

4 Understanding the Outside World: Customers and the Surrounding Environment — 53
- 4.1 Customer Analysis — 53
  - 4.1.1 Defining Customer Personas — 54
  - 4.1.2 Uncovering Underlying Customer Needs — 57
  - 4.1.3 Customer Problem Validation — 70
- 4.2 Environment Analysis — 71
  - 4.2.1 The Microenvironment — 72
  - 4.2.2 The Macroenvironment — 78
- References — 82

5 Outside-In: Defining the CX-Centric Business DNA—The Why, How, and What of a Start-Up — 85
- 5.1 Why? — 86
  - 5.1.1 Mission — 86
  - 5.1.2 Vision — 87
- 5.2 How? — 87
  - 5.2.1 Business Model — 88
  - 5.2.2 Brand Identity — 98
  - 5.2.3 Organisational Goal Setting — 104
  - 5.2.4 Leadership Culture — 106
- 5.3 What? — 109
  - 5.3.1 Customer Solution — 110
  - 5.3.2 Go-to-Market Approach — 114
  - 5.3.3 Ideation Techniques for Customer Solutions and G2M Strategy — 120
- References — 127

6 Inside-Out: Testing, Implementation, and Communication of Experience Elements — 133
- 6.1 Testing — 133
  - 6.1.1 Usability Testing — 134
  - 6.1.2 A/B Testing — 135

	6.2	Implementation	139
		6.2.1 Customer Solutions and Go-to-Market Strategy	139
		6.2.2 Feedback Loop	143
	References		144
7	**Future Considerations**		147
	Reference		149

Your Key Takeaways from the Book 151

Appendix: Definitions of Customer Experience 152

References 152

About the Authors

Thomas Suwelack is a part-time professor of digital customer experience at Brand University of Applied Sciences in Hamburg since October 2018. He is also the founder and CEO of 21done—a digital start-up focusing on empowering individuals to grow as a person. After graduating in business administration and completing his doctorate in marketing at the University of Muenster, he worked several years as a management consultant for multinational corporations operating in various industries.

Feng Xia Ang is the co-founder and Chief Product Officer of 21done. She holds a Bachelor of Business Management degree from the Singapore Management University and an M.A. in Brand Innovation from the Brand University of Applied Sciences. After her studies, she went on to fulfil her passion for entrepreneurship by embarking on the start-up founding journey alongside Thomas Suwelack of building a purposeful digital platform for personal growth.

Manuel Stegemann is a tenured professor at the Bielefeld University of Applied Sciences (Germany). He primarily represents the fields of consumer psychology and marketing. Before moving to Bielefeld, he worked for 3 years as a professor of marketing and statistics at the Kiel University of Applied Sciences (Germany). He is passionate about behavioral economics and consumer decision-making. He also enjoys delving into the new opportunities that data science brings to marketing. He studied psychology and holds a PhD in business administration. He gained 5 years of industry experience working for two management consultancies.

List of Figures

Fig. 2.1	Components of micro-and macro-experiences (adapted from Duerden et al., 2015)	7
Fig. 2.2	Types of customer experiences (adapted from Rossman & Duerden, 2019, p.50)	8
Fig. 2.3	Stages in the development of companies with the example of Starbucks (adapted from Pine & Gilmore, 2019)	13
Fig. 2.4	Driving forces of the experience economy	14
Fig. 2.5	Five phases of development towards the experience-centric organisation (adapted from Clatworthy, 2019)	18
Fig. 2.6	Comparison between a customer-centric and experience-centric organisation (adapted from Clatworthy, 2019, p. 34)	19
Fig. 2.7	NPS formula	25
Fig. 3.1	The start-up Madlibs (adapted from Founder Institute)	37
Fig. 3.2	Dos and do nots of a pitch deck	39
Fig. 3.3	Key points to include in a pitch deck according to venture capitalists and successful start-ups (adapted from Cayasso, 2019)	40
Fig. 3.4	Ten essentials for a pitch deck (adapted from Dirk Lehmann and Partners 2021)	41
Fig. 3.5	Problem description by 21done	42
Fig. 3.6	Solution description by 21done	43
Fig. 3.7	USP description by 21done	43
Fig. 3.8	Business model of 21done	44

List of Figures

Fig. 3.9	The TAM SAM SOM approach (adapted from Chi, 2021)	45
Fig. 3.10	Market opportunity description by 21done	45
Fig. 3.11	Team description by 21done	47
Fig. 3.12	Ask description by 21done	47
Fig. 3.13	Pitch deck storyline template	48
Fig. 3.14	The customer experience framework	50
Fig. 4.1	Overview of segmentation variables (adapted from Kotler & Armstrong, 2014)	54
Fig. 4.2	Customer persona template with example	56
Fig. 4.3	Empathy map canvas (Gray, 2017)	58
Fig. 4.4	The limbic map (Häusel, 2011)	59
Fig. 4.5	The five why technique, also known as laddering	61
Fig. 4.6	Customer journey mapping with example (adapted from Risdon, 2012)	63
Fig. 4.7	Overview of research methods and data sources (adapted from Sarstedt & Mooi, 2019)	65
Fig. 4.8	Overview of primary research methods	65
Fig. 4.9	Porter's five forces framework to analyse important aspects of the microenvironment (adapted from Porter, 1979)	73
Fig. 4.10	PESTEL framework to analyse the macroenvironment. The list of details is not exhaustive and should be supplemented in the specific individual case (cf. Aguilar, 1967)	79
Fig. 5.1	CX at the core of company DNA	86
Fig. 5.2	Business model canvas (adapted from Strategyzer, 2020)	89
Fig. 5.3	Comparison of revenue models	92
Fig. 5.4	The lean canvas (adapted from Maurya, 2010)	94
Fig. 5.5	The Amazon flywheel (adapted from Bezos, 2001)	96
Fig. 5.6	Elements of the flywheel: ten types of innovation (adapted from Keeley et al. 2013; Kylliäinen, 2019)	97
Fig. 5.7	The brand steering wheel (adapted from Esch, 2017)	99
Fig. 5.8	The brand identity prism (adapted from Kapferer, 2012)	102
Fig. 5.9	Stimulus organism response model for structuring goals (adapted from Bruhn, 2018, p.36)	105
Fig. 5.10	Values of 21done's corporate culture	107
Fig. 5.11	Principles to stimulate an entrepreneurial culture at 21done	108
Fig. 5.12	The platform framework	110
Fig. 5.13	Added value of platform companies (adapted from Choudary et al., 2016)	111

Fig. 5.14	The touchpoint template (adapted from Rossman & Duerden, 2019)	114
Fig. 5.15	The hubspot marketing flywheel (adapted from Hubspot, 2021)	115
Fig. 5.16	Volume, quality, value, and cost targets of digital communication tools (adapted from Chaffey and Ellis-Chadwick, 2019, p.157)	117
Fig. 5.17	Content types along degree of emotion and customer journey (adapted from Smart Insights, 2014)	118
Fig. 5.18	Sample structure for a product or service brainstorming session (adapted from Kreutzer & Land, 2017, p.57)	122
Fig. 5.19	The design thinking process (adapted from Nielsen Norman Group, 2016)	123
Fig. 5.20	Prototyping methods in the context of website creation (adapted from Traynham, 2019)	125
Fig. 5.21	SCAMPER techniques and examples	127
Fig. 6.1	Basic sequence of an A/B test (adapted from Stegemann & Suwelack, 2020)	137
Fig. 6.2	Overview of typical application fields for A/B tests (adapted from Stegemann & Suwelack, 2020)	138
Fig. 6.3	Typical process of A/B testing and multivariate testing (adapted from Stegemann & Suwelack, 2020)	139
Fig. 6.4	Feature priority matrix (adapted from Valuy, 2020)	140

1

Introduction

Digitisation has rendered the days of information asymmetry and race-to-the-bottom price competition obsolete; companies and consumers are simply a click away from detailed price and product comparisons, making it challenging for brands to justify higher price premiums for similar products. In this increasingly competitive market environment, how do successful brands continue to differentiate themselves and achieve a competitive positioning?

Consumer behaviour is continually evolving. Customer experience (CX) is becoming the next battlefield of businesses and *will overtake price and product as the key brand differentiator* (Wladawsky-Berger, 2018). While consumers have not completely moved away from price evaluation, the value derived is no longer just a comparison of the quality to price but also the customer experience. A cup of Starbucks coffee is worth its value, not only as a result of the quantity or quality of the product but the experience. Based on research, customer experience is strongly correlated to not only customer satisfaction but a wide spectrum of metrics, including share of wallet, loyalty, customer lifetime value and positive word of mouth. To put it simply, customer experience is a significant growth lever that cannot be undermined. It is time for companies to recognise and commit to managing their CX.

Since creating strong customer experience has and will become an important objective for many companies due to its positive influence on business metrics, the question is no longer whether companies should create strong customer experiences but *how to do it?* Due to the increasing pertinence of the topic of customer experience, a plethora of studies and literature on customer experience is available for a comprehensive exploration and understanding of the subject. In particular, the book focuses on start-ups due to their exceptionally high failure rate; nine in ten start-ups do not end up successful (Bryant, 2020). Moreover, there is a lack of a holistic framework which can support business practitioners in the actual implementation of a customer experience-centric organisation. Hence, this book seeks to consolidate and synthesise both theoretical and practical knowledge to design an applied framework that is backed by scientific research.

To achieve the intended goal, the book is structured as follows. The book begins with a definition of customer experience to set the scope and context of the book and discusses the importance of customer experience management in today's world. Following that, a comprehensive step-by-step customer experience framework aimed at guiding start-ups to create a CX-centric organisation is introduced and elaborated in detail, covering both explanations and applications of theoretical concepts and practitioner tools. Last but not least, the book ends with several points for future consideration and the main takeaways.

The book adds significant value to the field of business management. Firstly, on the specific subject of CX, it bridges the gap between practice and research by aligning practitioner knowledge with academic theories. Secondly, the book consolidates the existing knowledge and provides an up-to-date understanding of the topic of CX for academics or business managers to have a comprehensive overview. Thirdly, the book provides a structured framework and concrete tools for practitioners to apply in their existing business operations to achieve customer experience centricity and improve their business performance. While the focus is primarily on start-ups, most of the frameworks and tools can also be applied to the more established companies.

References

Bryant, S. (2020). *How many startups fail and why?* Accessed September 12, 2021, from https://www.investopedia.com/articles/personal-finance/040915/how-many-startups-fail-and-why.asp

Wladawsky-Berger, I. (2018). Customer experience is the key competitive differentiator in the digital age. [Blog] *The Wall Street Journal*. Accessed July 28, 2021, from https://www.wsj.com/articles/customer-experience-is-the-key-competitive-differentiator-in-the-digital-age-1524246745

2

Concept, Relevance, and Management of CX

Whether an organisation is consciously orchestrating customer experiences or not, customer experiences are being actively created every day; the difference lies in the decision to manage them. Prior to committing the organisation to creating strong customer experience, it is of great importance to first gain an adequate understanding of the concept and its significance. As such, this chapter aims to provide a theoretical explanation of CX and its related concepts to answer the following questions:

- What is CX?
- Why is CX important?
- How can an organisation manage its CX?

2.1 Concept of CX

CX is not a new term and certainly not a standalone concept. A dive into literature reveals a multitude of perspectives taken to define CX, many of which include references to other marketing and management concepts. Since CX is a broad and multidimensional concept, it is important to begin with a clear definition.

2.1.1 Definition

There is no one right way to define CX, but it is crucial to ensure that the employed definition covers a comprehensive perspective of the concept to facilitate a holistic coverage and discussion of the topic. While there exist multiple definitions, they mostly overlap and complement in their description of CX and do not contradict[1] (Jain et al., 2017; De Keyser et al., 2015; Lemon & Verhoef, 2016; Gartner, n.d.; Bordeaux, 2021). As such, a synthesised version has been put together to encapsulate the concept in its entirety:

Customer experience is the ***customer's*** ***overall perception*** of a brand, including ***cognitive, emotional, physical, sensorial, spiritual, and social responses*** to ***interactions*** throughout the ***customer journey*** which brings about significant impact on ***business performance***.

Based on this definition, it is clear that CX should be

- Managed from the customer point of view
- Analysed from a holistic and multidimensional perspective
- Focused on experience elements at touchpoints where customer interactions take place
- A focus for companies
- Measured and continually optimised

2.1.2 Experience Types

Customer experiences come in different forms, but every experience constitutes three phases, anticipation, participation and reflection, in which customer interactions with a company's experience elements take place (Duerden et al., 2015). See Fig. 2.1 for an overview of experience types.

The *anticipation* phase is where customers develop expectations for the later use of a particular service or product. In this phase, e.g. customers can be making the necessary preparations such as researching for information on the company website. Next, the *participation* phase is where

---

[1] Appendix: Definitions of customer experience.

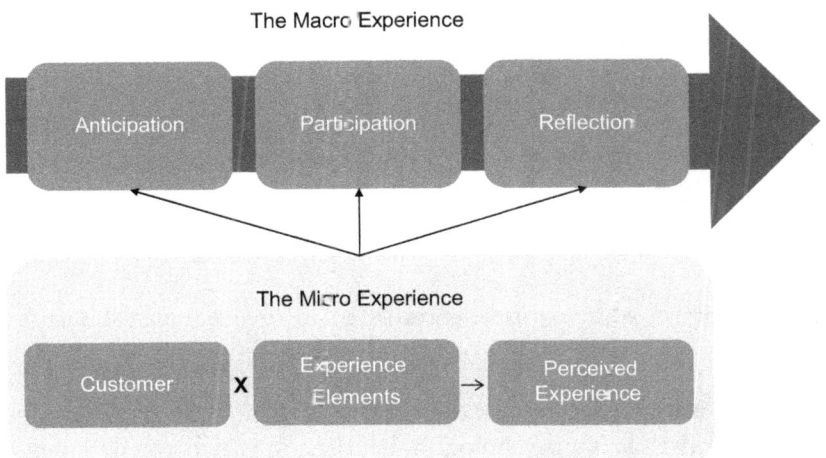

Fig. 2.1 Components of micro- and macro-experiences (adapted from Duerden et al., 2015)

the customers interact or use the product or service. It is important to note that the experience in the participation phase is heavily influenced by the anticipation phase as customers have a pre-expectation before the actual participation and any disappointments can lead to an undesirable customer experience. Since every experience is based on previously defined expectations, no unrealistic expectations should be stirred up by the company. Lastly, the *reflection* phase is highly cognitive, where customers holistically evaluate their entire customer experiences based on their past encounters, personal opinions, third party opinions and the interactions to arrive at an overall judgment or experience. The cumulation of the interactional experiences, also known as micro-experiences, is then referred to as the macro-experience (Duerden et al., 2015). These macro-experiences are important in influencing subsequent purchases as they are stored in the brain for the long term and can be referenced to when making a purchase decision. As such, it is important for companies to design strong micro-experiences through diverse experience elements, which will create strong positive macro-experiences. This will in turn lead to positive anticipation, which is a signficant deciding factor for subsequent purchases, influencing satisfaction, loyalty and revenue growth. In

Experience Types	Prosaic	Mindful	Memorable	Meaningful	Transformational
Mental Processes	Autopilot	Effortful Mental Engagement	Emotional Engagement	Discovery	Change
Frequency and Impact	Frequency				Impact
Engagement	System 1 Thinking			System 2 Thinking	
Emotional Engagement	Physical Pleasures				
		Higher Pleasures			
				Gratifications	

Fig. 2.2 Types of customer experiences (adapted from Rossman & Duerden, 2019, p. 50)

addition, it is important to take the "Peak-End-Rule" into consideration. The Peak-End-Rule is a psychological heuristic in which people judge an experience mainly based on how they felt at its peak and the end of the experience. It represents a highly relevant psychological concept to capture very important influences on the macro-experience (Strijbosch et al., 2019; Kahneman & Tversky, 2000). This concept assumes that the most intense micro-experiences, as well as the last micro-experience, influence the macro-experience the most. As such, when companies design experience elements, it is important to place extra emphasis on creating a peak and a positive end to increase the likelihood of a strong customer experience.

In order to create the intended customer experience, it is important for companies to understand the various types of micro-experiences and their characteristics. According to Rossman and Duerden (2019), experiences can be classified into five main types: prosaic, mindful, memorable, meaningful and transformational. In Fig. 2.2, we show important characteristics of these five types.

Prosaic Experiences
Prosaic is defined as "everyday, ordinary" and prosaic experiences are the most frequent experiences that customers have. These experiences trigger a low level of mental processing.

Kahneman and Tversky (2000) distinguish in their worldwide bestseller "Fast Thinking, Slow Thinking" between two types of thinking:

system 1 and 2. System 1 comprises cognitive thought processes that run largely unconsciously and very quickly and result in automatic, spontaneous behaviour (autopilot). An example would be adding 2 + 2. This system requires very little cognitive effort. In comparison, system 2 (pilot) requires very high cognitive performance. System 2 operates slowly and sluggishly, but is always required for more complex tasks, such as multiplying 13 by 11 or driving a car in a crowded pedestrian zone. Prosaic experiences run on system 1 thinking and do not or hardly reach the customer's consciousness or offer any apparent added customer value when viewed in isolation. Prosaic experiences are also usually lower in impact. Thus, these experiences are not used to provide competitive differentiation. Nevertheless, they should certainly not be overlooked, especially when it comes to activities that take place to enable or lead to a key activity such as a purchase transaction. Examples include parking at the supermarket or paying in the online store. Here, the focus of the provider should be on simplifying these processes as much as possible, e.g. by installing clearly understandable parking signs, so that the customer can stay in system 1 or autopilot mode. On the other hand, if they have to switch to system 2 or pilot mode due to the occurrence of complications (e.g. because parking signs are missing), the risk of negative customer experiences can increase. While prosaic experiences are not designed for customers to have an impactful impression, if designed well, they can help to reduce the need for unnecessary mental processes, which can lower the likelihood of poor customer experiences (Rossman & Duerden, 2019).

Mindful Experiences
Unlike prosaic experiences, mindful experiences require the *active or conscious cognitive engagement* with the element of experience. System 2 is engaged at a low intensity, and mental processes are activated. Mindful experiences are important to capture the attention of customers. To create such experiences, companies could look into injecting novelty to help break the monotony and increase mindfulness of the experience. However, it is important to note that repeated novelty can diminish its intended effects and should be used strategically and sparingly. An example would be the safety instructions on the airplane. In order to have airline

passengers listen in the first place, their cognitive attention must be gained. This is often attempted through the use of humour or unique formats such as singing and dancing (Rossman & Duerden, 2019).

Memorable Experiences
Memorable experiences, on the other hand, are experiences that stand out in one's memory. Such experiences are important for companies to leave a lasting impression on their customers, whether to support decision-making processes for the first or subsequent purchases. Memorable experiences require emotional engagement from customers. In addition, companies also need to strategically evoke positive emotions from customers while ensuring that it does not lead to a connecting fear or negative memory. For instance, Disney theme parks avoid the use of public announcements for lost-child situations as it can lead to anxiety and fear among visitors. Instead, they have a well-crafted plan which aims to calm the child with toys and games while at the same time leverage on coordinated efforts among personnel to search for the parents (Rossman & Duerden, 2019).

Meaningful Experiences
Like memorable experiences, meaningful experiences require emotional involvement but have an even greater impact on customer behaviour; new discoveries are made about oneself or a certain subject through the interaction with a company. Many pioneering companies, such as Tesla or Airbnb, enable meaningful customer experiences with their innovative offerings, e.g. steering electric cars for a more sustainable future and redefining travel with a local touch, respectively.

To create high involvement experiences, companies need to look into multiple ways of engaging customers through stimulating cognitive processing such as co-creation (Rossman & Duerden, 2019). Co-creation between customers and companies is a modern approach of product development and marketing where customers participate alongside the company in the process of new idea generation (Ind & Coates, 2013). A high involvement experience that supports co-creation is common for brands that offer personalisation. For instance, the "Nike by You" collection is a customisable shoe product line which allows customers to personalise the design of the shoes according to their preferences (Nike, 2021). By undergoing the process, customers are highly engaged both cognitively and emotionally, increasing their sense of attachment for the brand and the shoes. In addition, due to the meaningful value of products, services or touchpoints, companies should also look into leveraging on revenue to enable customers to share the new, positive insights and experiences with others (Rossman & Duerden, 2019).

Transformational Experiences
Lastly, transformational experiences happen extremely rarely and leave deep traces on consumers. In addition to reflection, emotion and discovery, a significant shift in the consumer's psychology must be triggered. This experience usually leads to a shift in perspectives, attitudes or behaviour and can be evoked by an incident or inspirational speeches such as a motivational TedTalk. However, it must be considered that these experiences can be subjective; a specific TedTalk may trigger a transformational experience in one person but only a mindful experience for another person due to their differing personal situations and backgrounds (Rossman & Duerden, 2019).

In addition, transformational experiences usually revolve around novel experiences. Novelty relates to how extraordinary the interaction feels to the customer. Often, companies looking to enhance their customer experience strategy will research on best practices and existing tactics employed by competitors. While this can certainly help companies to match up to the industry standards, it does not help them gain a competitive edge over the others (Edwards, 2014). As such, it is also crucial for companies to look into differentiating their customer experience by designing customer experiences that are unique and novel in such a way that consumers will remember and create unique associations of the company or brand in their minds (Dwivedi, 2018).

2.2 Relevance of CX

In this information-rich era fuelled by digitisation, customers can easily access tens of thousands of brands providing solutions to a single problem, many of which are almost identical in their products and pricing. How can businesses differentiate themselves amongst their rivals to win customers? The answer to this lies in the one thing which successful companies in this current digital age provide: *strong customer experiences*. CX has become the pulse of many businesses due to its positive impacts on corporate success and will continue to be. In this chapter, the relevance of CX in today's world will be further explained.

2.2.1 The Experience Economy

Experience trumps ownership. Consumers are no longer purchasing products and services for the sake of owning them but to gain the experiences that come with them: what can be done with the product, what it implies about the customer, and what they can share about the experience (D'Entremont, 2020). While this trend was initially driven by the millennials, a general shift in consumer values has been observed across various generations. This does not mean that companies selling products and services should start to sell experiences such as theatrical plays, but rather suggests a need for them to focus on orchestrating strong customer experience through customer interactions with their brand, products and services.

Consumer needs have shifted along with the experience economy. Strong customer experiences have now become a part of consumer expectations (Salesforce, 2020). This change in consumer sentiment implies a need for all companies to discover new ways of interacting with their customers. Companies who are able to recognise this shift and adapt in time will be able to experience the positive effects of higher perceived value, satisfaction, loyalty, word of mouth and revenue growth which come as a result of providing strong customer experiences (Tarkoff & Krigsman, 2019).

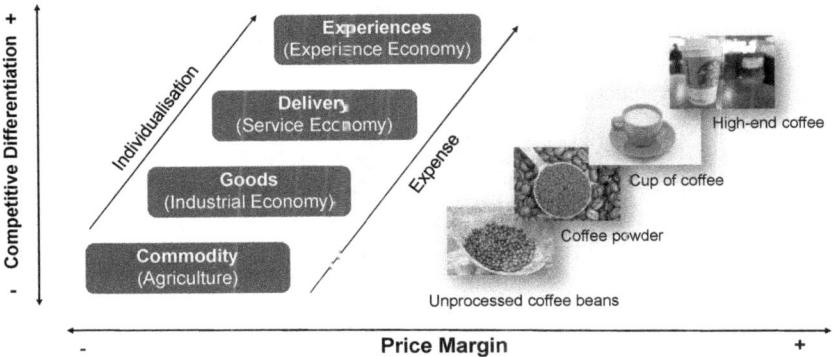

Fig. 2.3 Stages in the development of companies with the example of Starbucks (adapted from Pine & Gilmore, 2019)

Pine and Gilmore described customer experience as the highest level of corporate development in their pioneering book "The Experience Economy" in 1999. Customer experience is seen as the next stage of development after the "commodity", "goods", and "services" stages. In their opinion, the customer experience will continue to hold the highest status, reaffirming the current and future importance of CEM. Figure 2.3 shows the different stages.

The Starbucks example in Fig. 2.3 also shows that only those who are able to provide the best customer experience can charge a price premium for higher margins, highlighting the influence of customer experience on profitability.

According to Clatworthy (2019), the development of the "experience economy" or customer experience as a central corporate key performance indicator (KPI) can be seen as a logical outcome of four forces (see Fig. 2.4). In other words, the emergence of the experience economy was inevitable due to the interplay of the forces described below.

The increasing competition which has been massively intensified by digitisation (more and more providers vying for the consumer favour) pushes companies to find a differentiation for themselves by providing better customer experiences as experience is a type of economic offering that is challenging to replicate (Pine & Gilmore, 1999). In addition, the brand economy has also conditioned the experience economy as

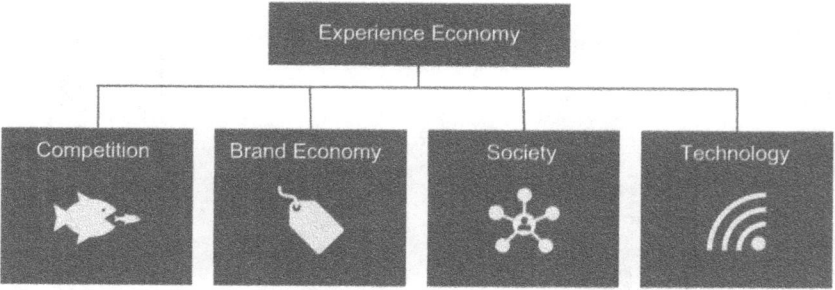

Fig. 2.4 Driving forces of the experience economy

numerous companies have had great success with their strategy of deep psychological penetration of target group-specific purchase motives. Good examples of this are companies such as Apple (stands for lifestyle, not computers) or Nike (whose slogan "Just do it" is intended to give customers strength), which have made customer experience the reason-to-be of their brands. The urge to experience, which is expressed in the quote by the Danish philosopher Soren Kierkegaard, "Life is not a problem to be solved, but a reality to be experienced", is representative of the third force, society. This drive to experience is particularly strong in Generations Y (also known as Millennials) and Z. In addition, the phenomenon of post-materialism is observed in the more advanced societies where a shift in values have been observed, from focusing on materialist goals such as economic growth, material success and security to values related to self-expression and quality of life, including work life balance, gender equality and environment protection (Inglehart, 2007). This shift fuels the experience economy as more attention is given to experiences and emotions, and less emphasis is placed on material success and ownership. In addition, the society is becoming more affluent and sees improved socio-economic conditions. According to Maslow's well-known pyramid of needs, higher economic success has also enabled more and more people to satisfy their basic needs and to increasingly strive for higher level pursuits such as psychological and self-actualising needs (Maslow, 1943). The latter can be addressed much better by an experience-centred economy than by commodity- or product-centred economies (Pine & Gilmore, 2019). In today's world, advancements in technologies also open the doors to new genres of experiences such as virtual reality, face recognition and personalisation (Pine & Gilmore, 1998), which increases consumer exposure and access to more experiences over time.

2.2.2 Customer Experience and Corporate Success

Customer experience is a huge determinant of corporate growth due to its significant impact on important KPIs such as customer satisfaction, revenue growth and loyalty. Its importance should certainly not be undermined.

The case of Airbnb provides an examplary proof of the relationship between customer experience and corporate success. Airbnb's consistent focus on providing strong customer experiences has resulted in high satisfaction and NPS values (NPS of 74 in 2019), which supported the company's growth to a billion-dollar global player within a few years. The company's strong focus on customer experience has deep roots in the DNA of its founders, as the following example illustrates (Clatworthy, 2019, p. 14): In the apartment rented out by the founders during Airbnb's formative years, guests always found a small pile of coins for the purchase of a subway ticket next to their beds. This purchase was a difficult undertaking for strangers, who often only carried bills, so this gesture was highly appreciated by guests and created an extremely positive customer experience. This empathy and pragmatic helpfulness of the founders then manifested itself in a customer experience-centric corporate DNA. Positive customer experiences could be created not only when *using* an accommodation rented via Airbnb's platform, but already during the accommodation booking process by focusing on beautiful photos of the apartment to be rented. To maximise the great customer experiences, clear instructions were also provided to the landlords on how these photos had to look or not look.

In addition, authors such as Pine and Gilmore (2019) also postulate that in times of interchangeable services, customers no longer use the price-quality ratio for their purchase decision but rather the (anticipated) price-experience ratio. In other words, customers tend to sum up in their minds the (positive and negative) experiences they have or are likely to have before, during and after purchasing a company service at a certain price, rather than merely paying attention to the quality of the service. This implies a change of perspective for companies: from product and service orientation to a focus on the psychology of the customer.

This change in perspective will be illustrated by a more detailed example of Starbucks. If the more psychologically-oriented price-experience ratio is not a key factor influencing the purchase decision—how else could a café latte from Starbucks at a price of 4.99 € be justified when a similar product priced at half the price can be found just a few metres from the Starbucks branch? Starbucks was founded in Seattle in 1971. However, it was not until the merger between Il Giornale, a company focused on unique customer experiences, and Starbucks in 1987 that the number of Starbucks cafés increased from 2 in 1986 to 1074 in 1996 (Karthik & Dixit, 2015, p. 1f). The objective of the former Starbucks CEO, Howard Schultz, was to implement the flair of Italian coffee bars that existed at Il Giornale in the Starbucks cafés as well. This was to be achieved through intensively trained baristas who celebrate the preparation of the coffee and at the same time ensure high product quality. A consistent focus on the customer experience should also be expressed in an exceptional choice of location and bar-like light dimming. Likewise, contact with the service staff at the checkout should be as pleasant and personal as possible ("Can I have your name please"?).

Schultz's experience-centered philosophy had proven to be successful: By simply wearing a white Starbucks cup and speaking the company's invented Italian lingua franca, customers identified themselves as belonging to a group of successful people with hip, urban tastes and an appreciation for the finer things in life. In flaunting their grande lattes, customers signaled that they were better than others—cooler, richer, and more sophisticated (Simon, 2009, p. 7). Among other things, Starbucks justifies its higher prices with these lifestyle experiences of its customers, or in the words of Howard Schultz: "We are not in the business of filling bellies. We are in the business of filling souls".

Airbnb and Starbucks are examples of companies that have become successful as a result of their consistent focus on the customer experience. This is the path that every company must take, especially in today's increasingly competitive times. It must be taken into account that customer expectations, which are the basis of decision for the creation of positive and negative experiences are subjective and vary depending on the contextual situation. For example customers today expect increasingly individualised offers or offers that are more tailored to them. Likewise, the literature shows a direct positive correlation between customer experience and customer loyalty as well as consumer spending (Srivastava & Kaul, 2016), willingness to pay (Carù & Cova, 2003), purchase intention (Nasermoadeli et al., 2013), and stock market value (Gilliam, 2013).

The positive correlation between customer experience and corporate success outlined earlier indicates that it should assume a very important role in the target system of every company. The following statistics and results further suggest that companies should use customer experience as the key company KPI:

- According to a survey by Newman and McClimans (2019), more than two-thirds of marketing managers see customer experience as the key success factor for a company.
- The Wall Street Journal (2018) calls CX the most important competitive factor in the digital age.
- Brands with superior customer experience generate 5.7 times more revenue than competitors who have poorer customer experience (Dicso, 2017).
- According to Bain & Co. (2015), companies with a customer experience commitment experience revenue growth 4–8% higher than their competitors.
- Good customer experience is key in influencing brand loyalty. (Puthiyamadam and Reyes 2018)

2.3 Management of CX

Companies should strive beyond achieving being customer centric, to being customer experience-centric. Customer centricity and customer experience centricity may sound similar, but there is a fundamental difference between the two terms. In a customer experience-centric

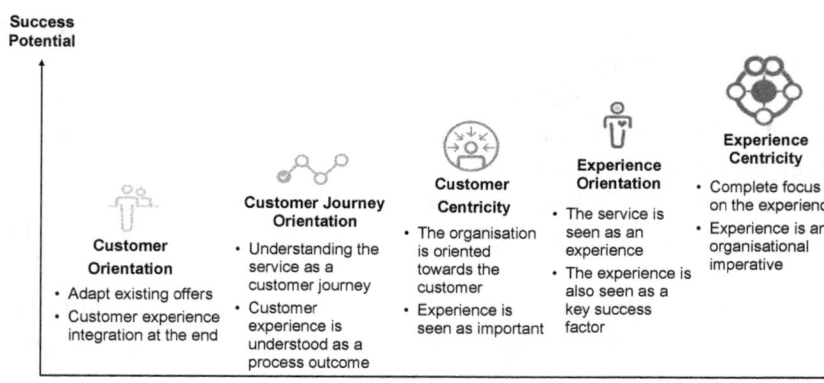

Fig. 2.5 Five phases of development towards the experience-centric organisation (adapted from Clatworthy, 2019)

company, the customer experience is the starting point of all their activities (What products or services do we need so that the customer feels…?). In contrast, in a customer-centric company, CX is understood and applied in a more shallow manner as developing consistent and pleasant experiences (Clatworthy, 2019). Customer experience in the customer experience-centric enterprise is an organisational imperative and must be thought about and designed proactively across all units of an enterprise. See Fig. 2.5 for an overview.

In today's highly competitive times, however, it is not a question of *whether* a company focuses on the customer and his experience but how *intensively* a company does so. Particularly in today's digital age, it is important for management to break down silos to an even greater extent and to align all corporate activities with the customer experience. According to Fig. 2.5, the experience-centric company has the greatest potential for success in this regard, thus every company should strive for this stage.

Instead of placing emphasis on the question "How can we increase revenue"? a truly CX-centric organisation would rather focus on finding the answers to the following strategic questions: What do we want our customers to feel? How can our organisation integrate into the lives of our customers? What competencies does the organisation possess which

2 Concept, Relevance, and Management of CX

Criteria	Customer Centricity	Experience Centricity
Focus	Customer satisfaction	Experiential desirability
Basic Philosophy	What do our customers want?	What do we want our customers to feel?
Basic Approach	Reactive	Proactive and experiential
Key Terms	Value proposition, segments, brand promise	Experiential value proposition, individuals, brand experience
Orientation	Services as products	Experiences delivered through services
Brand Orientation	Broadcasting a brand promise	Delivering a brand experience
CX is seen as	Something that supports customer satisfaction	The core source of value
Typical Perspective	"We need to offer something customers need"	"How does that suggestion impact our desired experience?"
Tactic to progress	Execute qualitative interviews (rather than quantitative)	Improve cultural interactions

Fig. 2.6 Comparison between a customer-centric and experience-centric organisation (adapted from Clatworthy, 2019, p. 34)

customers see value in? How can the organisation nuture and enhance these comptencies to maximise value creation for our customers? Can the organisation support our customer's jobs to be done? (De Keyser et al., 2015). To put it simply, a CX-centric organisation must proactively investigate how their customers use their products and services within their daily lives and how its offers can help them achieve their intended goals (Bettencourt et al., 2014). Figure 2.6 summarises the differences between customer and experience centricity. One person who has this mindset and has thus propelled his company above the status of just a customer-centric company is Jeff Bezos, former CEO of Amazon: "When we're at our best, we don't wait for external pressure. We are internally driven to improve our services [...] before we have to. We lower prices and increase value for customers before we have to. We invent before we have to".

At this point, the argument for creating a CX-centric organisation is clear and undoubted. The next question to raise is: how can a start-up manage its customer experience to bring about business success? Customer experience management (CEM) is "the systematic identification, prioritisation and incorporation of right set of clues at touchpoints across all the stages; designing and developing [experience elements] for experience creation; and measuring customer responses using appropriate performance metrics" (Jain et al., 2017, p. 652). Breaking this down, companies need to:

- Identify critical touchpoints across customer journeys that need to be managed.
- Design and develop experience elements by understanding the factors influencing CX.
- Measure customer responses.

The following sub-chapters will elaborate on the three key points which companies need to take into account for the creation of strong CX.

2.3.1 Understanding Touchpoints to Increase Customer Experience

Customer experiences are created on an interactional basis, i.e. when a customer interacts with the elements in various touchpoints along the customer journey. These elements should always be designed with their potential for creating positive customer experiences in mind and will be referred to as experience elements.

Since CX is highly influenced by customer interactions with various touchpoints, an understanding of touchpoints is a prerequisite for knowing where and how to implement effective experience elements. Touchpoints are contact points between the brand or company and customers which are present across the customer journey and serve specific purposes such as information collection and payment (Homburg et al., 2017; Lemon & Verhoef, 2016). Since CX is created on an interactional basis, these touchpoints are the gateway to facilitating the formation of experiences and must be identified and managed. To effectively manage touchpoints, it is important to understand the control, nature, and stage of each touchpoint.

Control

The touchpoint control can be understood by asking: *who controls the contact point?* In general, touchpoints can be classified into company-owned and non-company-owned. Company-owned touchpoints are those which are designed and implemented by the company while non-company-owned are those which are controlled by external parties such as customers and competitors (De Keyser et al., 2020). Company-owned touchpoints such as company website, customer services and employees need to be identified and analysed as the companies have strong influences on these and can use them to orchestrate strong and coherent CX for their customers.

On the other hand, companies should not overlook non-company-controlled touchpoints. Stakeholders are increasingly interconnected; the total customer experience is a function of many different experiences such as service delivery network (Tax et al., 2013) and outsourced activities (Kranzbühler et al., 2018). For instance, while Airbnb is able to deliver optimal performances on its platform and customer service, a huge part of the CX remains highly dependent on the actual service delivery by the property owners. Airbnb does not have a direct control on that, but it still holds the power to influence it by implementing certain measures such as vetting, reviews and post-stay customer service to reduce the risk of poor CX or increase the overall experience.

Nature
The nature of the touchpoint refers to the means by which the brand or company is represented at a particular touchpoint. Touchpoint can be represented by humans (e.g. customer care agent), digital (e.g. chatbot) to physical elements (e.g. retail store) (De Keyser et al., 2020). In the era of digitisation where digital and omni-channel marketing are gaining prominence, it is important for businesses to understand how the different nature of touchpoints can affect the CX delivery to inform their CX management strategies.

Stage
Following that, an understanding of the touchpoint stage, the phase of the customer journey in which the touchpoint is located, is crucial as customers exhibit different psychology and needs at different stages of the customer journey. The three main stages include pre-purchase, purchase, and post-purchase. The pre-purchase stage is the interaction phase before

a customer makes a purchase, consisting of need recognition, information search and evaluation in the customer journey. The purchase stage refers to the touchpoint interactions at the point of purchase, for instance, payment checkout. The post-purchase stage is the last phase that happens after a purchase, encompassing touchpoints such as after-sales service, return policy and actual product or service delivery (De Keyser et al., 2020; Lemon & Verhoef, 2016). While touchpoints need to be individually analysed and strategised, it is important to note that the customer experience should ultimately be managed as a whole and not simply by the individual touchpoints.

2.3.2 Context

CX can be perceived differently by every customer because every individual is innately unique and are exposed to different external environments which influence their perceptions (Sandström et al., 2008). As such, it is important for the company to identify the different contextual influences of its target groups for better customer segmentation and customer understanding to be able to create tailored customer experiences.

Individual
The individual context comprises factors such as emotions, cognitions, physical and economic factors. Firstly, an individual's emotions can influence his behaviour, e.g. a person who is happy is more receptive to trying new things, while a person who is sad is more likely to see things from a pessimistic lens. Secondly, a person's cognition can also greatly impact his perception and behaviour. For instance, a poor experience may result in the lack of trust and desire to re-engage with a company in the future (Verhoef et al., 2009), and a positive anticipation can lead to strong desires. Thirdly, physical factors such as an individual's health or ability can affect the way in which he interacts or purchases. Lastly, one's economic situation has a strong impact on his purchasing power and expectations, which ultimately affect his consumption behaviour (De Keyser et al., 2015). Hence, the same thing orchestrated by the company can be perceived differently as a result of the individual condition, highlighting

the importance of customer understanding and empathy at every touchpoint and stage of the customer journey (see Sect. 4.1).

Social
The social context refers to the social rules and norms followed by the consumers and the influences from their social network. Individuals no longer act in a social vacuum: they are in constant communication with their environment and social network. For instance, an individual's poor experience will not stay isolated to himself but most likely spread through his social network by word of mouth and sharing (De Keyser et al., 2020; Carù & Cova, 2015). As such, it is highly necessary to consider the influences of the social context and define strategies to not only mitigate in the case of poor experiences but also leverage the power of social influence in the case of a positive customer experience.

Market
The market context reflects the actors of the market with which the customers interact, including competitors, substitutes, and complements. The actions of these market actors can influence the customer behaviour. For instance, in the early days, customers were more brand loyal as a result of information asymmetry, which resulted in high perceived risk of switching (De Keyser et al., 2020). With the rise of actors like price aggregators and marketplaces, the level of transparency has increased, and customers can compare prices and information more easily and switch with reduced costs. In addition, competitors' actions such as new product launches or promotions can also impact consumer expectations. As such, understanding the market context (see Sect. 4.2.1: Microenvironment Analysis) can add value and knowledge to the management of CX.

Environmental
The environmental context refers to the macroenvironment of the customers, including factors that are political, economic, environmental, and technological in nature. The environmental context has a significant impact on consumer behaviour as every individual functions within a broader environment (De Keyser et al., 2020). For instance, the global COVID-19 pandemic has resulted in lower consumption levels due to

unstable economic conditions but a higher consumption level on necessities due to the stay-home phenomenon. In addition, the pandemic has also resulted in a shift in consumer behaviour towards the digital space. While it can be argued that customers may eventually revert to their old ways, it is undoubted that there is an increased openness and familiarity towards digital activities such as online shopping and learning (OECD, 2020). An up-to-date understanding of the environmental context (see Sect. 4.2.2: Macroenvironment Analysis) can help to inform CX planning and ensure a quick reaction to changes in market needs.

The chapter has provided a good understanding of the concept of CX and the important aspects which are necessary for CEM. CEM has the task of orchestrating the micro-customer experiences along the customer journey with the aim to maximise the macro-customer experience.

2.3.3 CX Measurement

How does one know if a company's CEM is successful? One cannot manage what one cannot measure. Even though the importance of CX has been established and understood, there is no one tool that provides a holistic measurement of CX. Since CX is a culmination of several concepts, measuring it requires a multi-method approach and cannot be centred around one single measure such as satisfaction or word of mouth. Instead, a combination of metrics will enable a more accurate measurement of CX initiatives and useful insights to inform strategic decisions (De Keyser et al., 2015). This chapter covers some of the most common and relevant metrics for the measurement of customer experience. We will discuss the following metrics and tools that can be employed by companies to measure the customer experience:

- Net Promoter Score
- Customer satisfaction
- Customer effort score
- Churn rate
- Share of wallet
- Sentiment analysis

The *Net Promoter Score (NPS)* value is commonly used in corporate practice as the "closest relative" of the customer experience, in addition to the measurement of sales figures or market share. To determine the NPS value, customers are asked the following question "On a scale of 0 to 10, how likely is it that you will recommend our company/product/service/brand to your friends and colleagues"? (Reichheld, 2003).

The NPS is then obtained by subtracting the proportion of promoters (those who answered 9 or 10) and the proportion of detractors (those who answered 0–6). Respondents who answered a score of 7 and 8 are referred to as neutrals. A positive NPS score indicates that the company has more customers willing to promote it than critics, while a negative NPS indicates that most customers are detractors, which signals a need to relook at the customer experience management strategy (see Fig. 2.7). In addition, it is also important to note that the NPS should be evaluated with the industry benchmarks in mind as well as to compare against the scores of competitors to understand the company's competitive position (Qualtrics, 2021). While the NPS is a simple and convenient tool in helping companies understand satisfaction, liking and advocacy, it is limited in providing further insights to drive strategic decisions and does not measure the outcome on business growth. As such, it should be accompanied by follow up questions to collect insights for optimisations, and other metrics to achieve a more comprehensive evaluation.

Another simple tool to measure customer experience is the *Customer Satisfaction Score (CSAT)*. The CSAT measures customer satisfaction with respect to not only a company but also purchase and interactions. To measure the CSAT, the question "How satisfied are you with your experience"? will be asked and respondents will answer on a scale (e.g. 1–7). The CSAT can then be calculated by summing up the number of satisfied

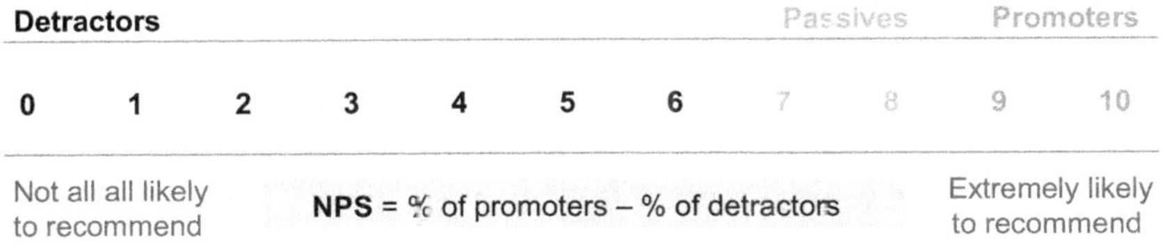

Detractors						Passives		Promoters	
0	1	2	3	4	5	6	7	8	9	10

Not all all likely to recommend   NPS = % of promoters – % of detractors   Extremely likely to recommend

Fig. 2.7 NPS formula

responses (e.g. scores of 5–7) and dividing by the total number of responses collected and multiplying by 100 to arrive at the percentage of satisfied customers (Birkett, 2021b). While the CSAT is less comprehensive than the NPS, it can be used to understand customer satisfaction at a specific moment, enabling companies to promptly address any identified issues. This breakdown of evaluation can be especially helpful in the identification and management of touchpoints or interactions which require optimisations.

Customer Effort Score (CES) is another popular metric which measures the ease of an experience. To calculate the CES, companies ask the question "On a scale of '1=very easy' to '10=very difficult', how easy was it to (intended experience)"? E.g. "On a scale of '1=very easy' to '10=very difficult', how easy was it to find what you are searching for on Airbnb"? The underlying belief of the CES is that customers are more likely to be loyal and less likely to churn if the experience made it easy for them to perform their jobs-to-be-done (Birkett, 2021a). The CES is usually conducted after completing an action, e.g. purchase and customer service call. To calculate the CES, all ratings for a particular action should be added and divided by the total number of responses for the particular action. The final score allows companies to assess how easy it is for their customers to perform the specific action, and a comparison with the scale will signal if there is a need to simply certain processes and to improve user-friendliness.

Unlike the first three metrics, which involve direct customer inputs and measure psychological constructs of the customer, the *Churn Rate* is calculated on the basis of actual customer behaviour. Customers churn, leave their interactions with the company and stop using the company services when they have poor customer experience. Measuring the churn rate is important as it helps companies understand if the customer experience is impacting the business growth. The churn rate can be calculated by dividing the number of customers lost by the number of total customers the company started with (Lindfors, 2019). Different time horizons, e.g. month, quarter or year, can be applied for evaluations that are more relevant to a specific time frame. The advantage of this metric lies in the fact that it is directly linked to the customer action and does not require further inferences or articulation. The churn rate does not provide actionable insights but serves a signalling purpose for companies to understand the behaviour of their customers. In addition, the use of it along with other metrics can help to identify the source of churn for mitigation.

The *Share of Wallet* represents the percentage of spending in a category that customers give to a brand (Keiningham et al., 2015). Companies can perform strongly in their customer satisfaction and NPS but continue to take up a small share of their customers' wallet as they do not take into account relative performance of competitors and the fact that customers use more than a single brand. In order to avoid being misled by the high satisfaction scores, the wallet allocation should be applied. Firstly, companies need to identify the companies or brands within the same product or service category which customers use. Secondly, an overall satisfaction or loyalty question should be asked to find out the performance of competing brands that each customer uses. Thirdly, a performance ranking value should be given to each brand for each customer based on the results from the earlier question. Next, calculate the share of wallet with the wallet allocation rule formula for each customer:

$$= \left(1 - \frac{rank}{number\ of\ brands + 1}\right) \times \frac{2}{number\ of\ brands}$$

The calculated score is the share of the wallet for the individual customer. To arrive at a company-level score, sum up the scores of all customers for a particular company and divide it by the number of customers. The final score reflects the relative percentage of customer spending on the company and its competitors. If the relative ranking is undesirable, the next step for companies to undertake is to carry out an analysis of purchase drivers, i.e. why companies use the brands they use and how the competing companies perform on these factors. By understanding the determinants of customer purchases and the relative performance of the company, companies can then leverage on these insights to decide where to allocate its precious resources to in order to win the shares of customers (Keiningham et al., 2015). While this metric is highly informative, it requires more time and effort for execution and is challenging to involve a representative sample. This metric is especially important for companies that compete in relatively saturated markets and offer highly substitutable products.

For the identification of qualitative sentiments, *Sentiment Analysis*, also known as opinion mining, is the process of identifying sentiments embedded in the text to understand consumer opinions, attitudes, and emotions towards a subject (Yousef et al., 2014), can be employed. Sentiment analysis is often used in social monitoring and feedback analysis to help companies efficiently detect customer issues from social media posts, reviews, and comments for timely management (Neri et al., 2012). A sentiment analysis conducted over a period of time can enable companies to understand not only their customer experience performance but also what and where they are performing well or undesirably in.

References

Bain & Co. (2015). Accessed June 25, 2021, from https://www.bain.com/insights/are-you-experienced-infographic/

Bettencourt, L. A., Lusch, R. F., & Vargo, S. L. (2014). A service lens on value creation: Marketing's role in achieving strategic advantage. *California Management Review, 57*(1), 44–66. https://doi.org/10.1525/cmr.2014.57.1.44

Birkett, A. (2021a). *What is Customer Effort Score (CES)?* Accessed July 14, 2021, from https://blog.hubspot.com/service/customer-effort-score

Birkett, A. (2021b). *What is Customer Satisfaction Score (CSAT)?* Accessed July 14, 2021, from https://blog.hubspot.com/service/customer-satisfaction-score?toc-variant-a=

Bordeaux, J. (2021). *What is customer experience? (and why it's so important)*. Accessed June 20, 2021, from https://blog.hubspot.com/service/what-is-customer-experience

Carù, A., & Cova, B. (2003). Revisiting consumption experience: A more humble but complete view of the concept. *Marketing Theory, 3*(2), 267–286. In: *Journal of Leisure Research, 47*(5), p. 601 (2015).

Carù, A., & Cova, B. (2015). Co-creating the collective service experience. *Journal of Service Management, 26*(2), 276–294.

Clatworthy, S. D. (2019). *The experience-centric organisation: How to win through customer experience*. Sebastopol: O'Reilly Media. Available from: ProQuest Ebook Central.

D'Entremont. (2020, March 23). *The experience economy: Millennials paving a new way forward for marketing*. Accessed July 12, 2021, from https://medium.com/the-forge-institute/the-experience-economy-millennials-paving-a-new-way-forward-for-marketing-fc508483e80

De Keyser, A., Verleye, K., Lemon, K. N., Keiningham, T., & Klaus, P. (2015). *A framework for understanding and managing the CX*. Marketing Science Institute Working Paper Series 2015, Report No. 15-121. Marketing Science Institute.

De Keyser, A., Verleye, K., Lemon, K. N., Keiningham, T., & Klaus, P. (2020). Moving the customer experience field forward: Introducing the touchpoints, context, qualities (TCQ) nomenclature. *Journal of Service Research, 23*. https://doi.org/10.1177/1094670520928390

Dicso, J. (2017, October 19). *Why personalization is key for retail customer experiences*.

Duerden, M. D., Ward, P. J., & Freeman, P. A. (2015). Conceptualizing structured experiences: Seeking interdisciplinary integration. *Journal of Leisure Research, 47*(5), 601.

Dwivedi, A. (2018). Brand experience and consumers' willingness-to-pay (WTP) a price premium: Mediating role of brand credibility and perceived uniqueness. *Journal of Retailing and Consumer Services, 44*. https://doi.org/10.1016/j.jretconser.2018.06.009

Edwards, G. (2014). *Creating a differentiated experience that customers actually enjoy*.

Gartner. (n.d.). *Customer experience. Gartner Glossary*. Accessed June 15, 2021, from https://www.gartner.com/en/information-technology/glossary/customer-experience

Gilliam, J. (2013, January 21). *The direct relationship between stock price and customer experience*. Accessed July 18, 2021, from https://www.ttec.com/blog/direct-relationship-between-stock-price-and-customer-experience

Homburg, C., Jozíc, D., & Kuehnl, C. (2017). Customer experience management: Toward implementing an evolving marketing concept. *Journal of the Academy of Marketing Science, 45*(3), 377–401.

Ind, N., & Coates, N. (2013). The meanings of co-creation. *European Business Review, 25*. https://doi.org/10.1108/09555341311287754

Inglehart, R. F. (2007). *Postmaterialism. Encyclopedia Britannica*. Accessed August 10, 2021, from https://www.britannica.com/topic/postmaterialism

Jain, R., Aagja, J., & Bagdare, S. (2017). Customer experience – a review and research agenda. *Journal of Service Theory and Practice, 27*(3), 642–662. https://doi.org/10.1108/JSTP-03-2015-0064

Kahneman, D., & Tversky, A. (2000). *Choices, values, and frames*. Cambridge University Press.

Karthik, D., & Dixit, M. R. (2015). *Starbucks 2017*. Accessed July 12, 2021, from https://hbsp.harvard.edu/home/

Keiningham, T., Aksoy, L., Williams, L., & Buoye, A. (2015). *The wallet allocation rule: Winning the battle for share*. Wiley.

Kranzbühler, A., Kleijnen, M., Morgan, R., & Teerling, M. (2018). The multi-level nature of customer experience research: An integrative review and research agenda. *International Journal of Management Reviews, 20*(2), 433–456.

Lindfors, S. (2019). *What customer churn is and how to calculate it*. Accessed July 14, 2021, from https://lumoa.me/blog/customer-churn-and-how-to-calculate-it

Lemon, K. N., & Verhoef, P. (2016). Understanding customer experience throughout the customer journey. *Journal of Marketing, 80*, 69–96.

Maslow, A. (1943). A theory of human motivation. *Psychological Review, 50*(4), 370–396.

Nasermoadeli, A., Kwek, L., & Maghnati, F. (2013). Evaluating the impacts of customer experience on purchase intention. *International Journal of Business and Management, 8*(6), 128–138.

Neri, D., Aliiprandi, C., Capeci, F., & Cuadros, M. (2012). *Sentiment analysis on social media*. https://doi.org/10.1109/ASONAM.2012.164

Newman, D., & McClimans, F. (2019). *Experience 2030: The future of customer experience EMEA*. https://www.sas.com/content/dam/SAS/documents/marketing-whitepapers-ebooks/third-party-whitepapers/en/futurum-experience-2030-emea-110977.pdf

Nike. (2021). *Nike by you*. Accessed July 15, 2021, from https://www.nike.com/nike-by-you

OECD. (2020). *Digital transformation in the age of COVID-19: Building resilience and bridging divides*. Digital Economy Outlook 2020 Supplement. OECD. www.oecd.org/digital/digital-economy-outlook-covid.pdf

Pine, B. J., & Gilmore, J. H. (1999). *The experience economy: Work is theatre & every business a stage*. Harvard Business Press.

Pine, J. P., & Gilmore, J. H. (2019). *The Experience Economy, With a New Preface by the Authors: Competing for Customer Time, Attention, and Money*. Harvard Business Review Press.

Puthiyamadam, T., & Reyes, J., (2018). *Experience is everything: Here's how to get it right*. https://www.pwc.com/us/en/zz-test/assets/pwc-consumer-intelligenceseries-customer-experience.pdf. Accessed 15 July 2021

Qualtrics. (2021). *What is Net Promoter Score (NPS)? Everything you need to know*. Accessed July 20, 2021, from https://www.qualtrics.com/uk/experience-management/customer/net-promoter-score/?rid=ip&prevsite=en&newsite=uk&geo=DE&geomatch=uk

Reichheld, F. F. (2003). The number one you need to grow. *Harvard Business Review, 12*, 47–54.

Rossman, J. R., & Duerden, M. D. (2019). *Designing experiences*. Columbia University Press. ProQuest Ebook Central. Accessed July 15, 2021, from https://ebookcentral.proquest.com/lib/brand-university/detail.action?docID=5613936

Salesforce. (2020). *What are customer expectations, and how have they changed?* Accessed July 12, 2021, from https://www.salesforce.com/resources/articles/customer-expectations/

Sandström, S., Edvardsson, B., Kristensson, P., & Magnusson, P. (2008). Value in use through service experience. *Managing Service Quality, 18*(2), 112–126.

Simon, B. (2009). *Everything but the coffee: Learning about America from Starbucks* (p. 7). University of California Press.

Srivastava, M., & Kaul, D. (2016). Exploring the link between customer experience-loyalty-consumer spend. *Journal of Retailing and Consumer Services, 31*, 277–286.

Strijbosch, W., Mitas, O., van Gisbergen, M., Doicaru, M., Gelissen, J., & Bastiaansen, M. (2019). From experience to memory: On the robustness of the peak-and-end-rule for complex, heterogeneous experiences. *Frontiers in Psychology, 10*, 1705. https://doi.org/10.3389/fpsyg.2019.01705

Tarkoff, R., & Krigsman, M. (2019). Customer experience and the experience economy. *Oracle and CXO Talk*. Accessed July 13, 2021, from https://www.cxotalk.com/video/customer-experience-experience-economy

Tax, S., McCutcheon, D. M., & Wilkinson, I. F. (2013). The Service Delivery Network (SDN): A customer-centric perspective of the customer journey. *Journal of Service Research, 16*(4), 454–470.

Verhoef, P. C., Lemon, K. N., Parasuraman, A., Roggeveen, A., Tsiros, M., & Schlesinger, L. A. (2009). Customer experience creation: Determinants, dynamics and management strategies. *Journal of Retailing, 85*(1), 31–41.

Wladawsky-Berger, I. (2018). Customer experience is the key competitive differentiator in the digital age. [Blog] *The Wall Street Journal*. Accessed July 28, 2021, from https://www.wsj.com/articles/customer-experience-is-the-key-competitive-differentiator-in-the-digital-age-1524246745

Yousef, A. H., Medhat, W., & Mohamed, H. (2014). Sentiment analysis algorithms and applications: A survey. *Ain Shams Engineering Journal, 5*. https://doi.org/10.1016/j.asej.2014.04.011

3

Starting a Start-Up

A start-up always begins with a business idea. For the idea to grow and come to life, several topics such as customer relevance and market potential need to be thoroughly analysed. Along with other crucial topics, these analyses will be structured and documented in a pitch deck. As soon as the entrepreneur receives positive feedback on his pitch deck, he may decide to create a start-up around his business idea. To increase the likelihood of creating a successful company, a structured approach, i.e. a step-by-step framework to create CX-centric start-ups is necessary. These three topics—initial idea, pitch deck and start-up framework—will be covered in this chapter.

3.1 The Founding Idea

Every company begins with an initial idea, which could arise from deliberate ideation or an organic inspiration. The greatest and most successful start-up ideas have three shared commonalities (Graham, 2012):

- Ideas are based on what the founders want and need.
- Founders should be able to build the ideas themselves.
- Ideas are often perceived as not worthy of doing by the masses.

In essence, a great start-up idea is one that the founder is passionate about, solves a real problem and has a certain level of complexity which increases the barriers to replication. There are countless ideas for companies to pursue, but companies have to focus and start somewhere. The following chapters provide some guiding questions and tools which can be employed to find this starting point.

The Founder's World
Quoting Steve Jobs (2007), "People say you have to have a lot of passion for what you're doing and it's totally true. And the reason is because it's so hard that if you don't, any rational person would give up. […] If you don't love it, you're going to fail. So you've got to love it, you've got to have passion". Building a start-up requires high commitment and is often an arduous endeavour. It requires strong resilience to persevere through challenging times. Without a burning desire and interest for the subject, one will struggle to get into a flow state and lack the stamina to continually push boundaries and stand back on his feet after failures. As such, it is important to build a start-up on a subject which the founder is passionate about, which could be a strong personal need or purpose. These can be uncovered by asking "what is a problem you face in life which you would pay for it to be solved"? and "what is your purpose in life"?

The Future World

> Live in the future, then build what's missing (Graham, 2012).

A successful business idea solves a customer problem, and sometimes it can be worthwhile to look beyond the existing problems to foresee future problems, which are opportunities of today. For instance, Perkins, the CEO of Canva, an online design platform, had the initial goal to "take the entire design ecosystem, integrate it into one page, and then make it accessible to the whole world", because she thought "that in the future it was all going to be online and collaborative and much, much simpler than these really hard tools [like Adobe and Microsoft]" (Gilchrist, 2020). With this projection and prediction in mind, Canva is now valued at $3.2 billion and has helped to create almost 2 billion designs in 190 countries.

The Present World
Regardless of how advanced the society is, there are always unmet customer problems and needs, but how can they be identified? To understand existing needs which are not solved or effectively solved, tools such as observations, interviews, and social media listening can provide insights into what problems people are facing. Existing solutions to problems can also be analysed to understand the reason for their ineffectiveness or failure and be optimised to become an improved product. From these insights, the founder can identify problems which he is passionate about solving and proceed to explore in more depth. In addition, the ideation techniques elaborated in Sect. 5.3.3 can also be employed to generate new initial ideas.

Entrepreneurs begin their start-up journey with a rough idea in mind. Section 3.2 will provide a framework to summarise the idea and its business potential in a comprehensive manner and from various perspectives.

3.2 The Start-Up Pitch

Ideas are like seeds; they are the starting point of a tree, but not all seeds end up as a tree. The success of their growth depends on their compatibility with the environment, the external conditions, and the nurturing process. Likewise, ideas need to address existing and relevant customer needs, be able to compete within the environment and be developed.

Furthermore, it is very common for founders to become hyper-focused on initial ideas at the expense of an important fact: A start-up founder's success is dependent on others buying into the start-up and the founder's vision. In other words, a start-up's success is contingent upon the founders' ability to pitch the value of who they are, what they are offering doing and why it matters.

Achieving important milestones like raising venture capital, sourcing top talent, and acquiring new customers all require the same skill—telling a story that makes someone say, "Heck, yeah"! (Founder Institute 2021a, b) Sometimes you have 10 min to make that happen; other times you only have 60 s. In any case, a founder's job is to clearly communicate why a given audience should care about his or her business. A founder should be well prepared for these situations. Fortunately, there are clear guidelines for preparing a pitch. In case a founder is given some time, he will make use of the pitch deck, which is like a visual business plan.

"The purpose of a presentation deck is to enable entrepreneurs to effectively tell the story of their business", says Bill Gurley (2015), general partner at Benchmark Capital. "In many ways it's like a structured scientific proof. You want to walk the listener through an argument as to why this is going to be an amazing business". Before attaining the opportunity to give a longer presentation, a founder is most likely given only a few seconds first to pitch the start-up. For this first introduction, there is another powerful tool that the founder should make use of: the structured one-sentence pitch. A great one-sentence pitch should bring the start-up into the next phase with an investor.

Both the short and long version should grab the audience's attention and elicit interest for the idea. The audience is not only investors but also employees and customers. While customers will not see the pitch deck itself, they will see the implementation of a well-written pitch deck within the business offers. It can be said that great pitches are thoughtfully contemplated, tested about a hundred times, refined after every round, for more substance, clarity, entertainment, and business logic. Fortunately, pitching is not an art but a skill that can be practiced over time.

In addition, pitch principles are not only applicable in business, but in many real-life situations for convincing others for one's own ideas and get more followers. Before moving to the pitch deck, the next chapter will start with a guideline for the one-sentence pitch, which should support the founder to get to the next stage where he is given more time to convince the audience.

3.2.1 One-Sentence Pitch

Start-up founders meet hundreds of people at various meetings, events, and conferences. They also, routinely, introduce themselves to complete strangers by email. In such situations, a founder has 1 min max to peak someone's curiosity. This situation is also called an elevator pitch, as it can quickly be recited to a stranger on an elevator ride.

This elevator pitch explains in simple language what the start-up does, who it serves and why it matters. The Madlibs pitch format by The Founder Institute (see Fig. 3.1) provides a structured tool for a one-sentence pitch construction: My company, (*name of company*), is developing (*a defined offering*) to help (*a defined audience*) (*solve a problem*) with (*secret sauce*) (Ressi, n.d.).

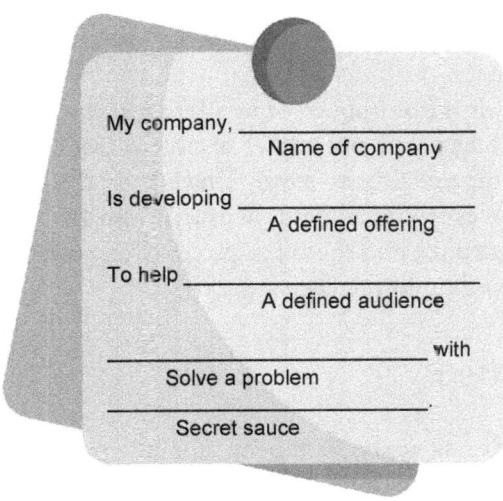

Fig. 3.1 The start-up Madlibs (adapted from Founder Institute)

- *Defined Offering:* The defined offering is a concise description of the idea which allows the audience to have a quick product reference, e.g. a fitness mobile app or a research software.
- *Defined Audience:* The defined audience is the target segment to whom the company will offer its initial idea to. The target segment can be identified by various segmentation variables such as demography, psychography, behaviour, and geography. For instance, university students specialising in social science studies.
- *Solve a Problem:* The problem is the customer need or pain you have identified amongst the defined audience, which your initial idea is focused on solving. This is extremely important as this is what the audience pays attention to. If they do not face the identified problem, the idea is irrelevant for them. E.g. to reduce the time needed to perform academic research. Hence, companies should begin to conduct initial interviews to get some first thoughts and opinions on whether the customer problem identified is relevant and who it is relevant for. The initially defined audience should be progressively refined as more information about the target market is uncovered.
- *Secret Sauce:* Lastly, the secret sauce is the distinct way in which the company aims to solve the problem. E.g. by providing a digital space to allow students to share access to different research sources and papers.

At this point, it is not important to already have the minute details of the business thought out but rather a clear direction, particularly the problem the company aims to solve. This is only the first version of the pitch, which serves to consolidate the initial idea for the company. It is not yet the perfect pitch and should be progressively refined with increased market understanding in the later steps.

3.2.2 Pitch Deck

Start-ups can choose to bootstrap by not relying on external capital. However, it is not always possible for the founders to have sufficient capital to grow the business in the long run. As such, it is strategic and natural for start-ups to look into funding opportunities. To be applicable for these programmes, companies need to sell their business idea and convince the investors of their business potential. An important resource in this process is the pitch deck.

A pitch deck is a visual presentation of a business providing an overview of the problem-solution approach, vision, and market opportunities. The objective of a founder is to precisely illustrate marketplace knowledge, business model and qualifications for execution. It is supposed to be presented in 5–10 min and 10–14 slides. These slides need to cover some standard topics that every investor is interested in before making an investment decision. In particular, the three main investor worries should be addressed in the pitch deck:

- Product Risk: Do you have a sustainable competitive advantage solving an unfulfilled need?
- Market Risk: Are you addressing a large, growing market?
- Execution Risk: Can your team "pull it off"?

A common mistake made by first-time founders is to provide too much detail. Jenny Lefcourt (2016), General Partner at Freestyle Capital, cautions early-stage founders against making this error: "What's really important is to not go into the weeds of all the details because what you're trying to do is give them enough information that they want more information. Your goal at meeting No. 1 is to get people interested enough that they want meeting No. 2". Figure 3.2 provides a summary of the dos and do nots of a pitch deck.

Dos	Don'ts
Use large fonts which are easy to read	Include unsubstantiated growth projections.
Include well designed charts, statistics, and graphics.	Provide excessive text or use tons of bullet points.
Label each slide (e.g., problem, solution, team).	Inflate your capabilities.

Fig. 3.2 Dos and do nots of a pitch deck

Structure and Content of a Pitch Deck

While there is no *one* approach for structuring a pitch deck, there are some shared beliefs across pitch experts and venture capital firms (Fig. 3.3).

In order to provide a consolidation of the "must-haves" for a pitch deck, the authors have included insights gained from pitching to multiple investors and mentors as well taking reference from many other founders' pitches to come up with the following overview of topics that must be included in any pitch deck (Fig. 3.4).

In the following, every key topic of a pitch deck will be elaborated on along with a few exemplary slides from the pitch deck of 21done (2020)—the start-up of two of the three authors of this book. Further slide examples can be accessed via Pitch Deck Coach.[1]

1. *Title page*: Put key visuals that represent the core idea of your business. Text should be minimal here. The core idea should be summarised in ten words or less and include your business name and logo. If the

	500 Startups	Guy Kawasaki	Sequoia Capital	NextView Ventures	Crowdfunder	Airbnb Pitch Deck
Slides	11	10	11	15+	12	13
Problem	✓	✓	✓	✓	✓	✓
Solution/Value Proposition	✓	✓	✓	✓	✓	✓
Market Validation			✓	✓		✓
Market Size	✓		✓	✓		✓
Business Model	✓	✓	✓	✓	✓	✓
Competition	✓	✓	✓	✓	✓	✓
Go To Market Plan	✓			✓	✓	✓
Founding Team	✓	✓	✓	✓	✓	✓
Traction and Milestones	✓	✓		✓	✓	
Fundraising	✓	✓	✓	✓	✓	✓

Fig. 3.3 Key points to include in a pitch deck according to venture capitalists and successful start-ups (adapted from Cayasso, 2019)

---

[1] https://pitchdeckcoach.com/pitch-deck-template#market-opportunity-slide

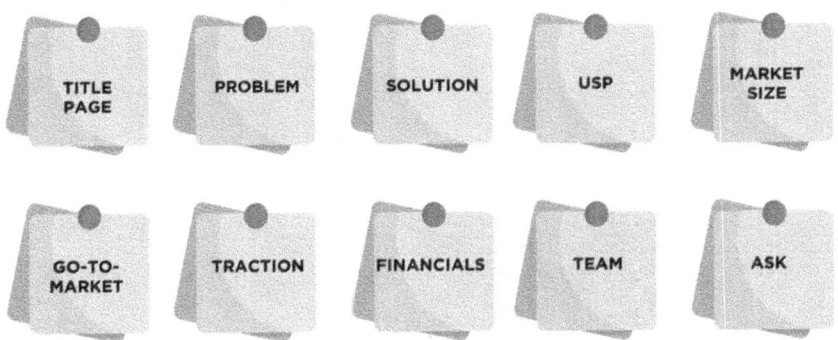

Fig. 3.4 Ten essentials for a pitch deck (adapted from Dirk Lehmann and Partners 2021)

pitch is supposed to be sent out rather than presented, it can make sense to add a one sentence below the key claim. Lastly, the name and contact information of the presenter or CEO should be put on this slide.

2. *Problem:* First and foremost, every start-up needs to solve a real problem. For this, a lot of empathy with the persona is required. The persona in the context of a new start-up refers to customer number one. Who is this customer number one? Which problem is it? Why is it so painful? The problem must be precisely defined. The problem description can take the form of a story that includes facts about the problem as well as emotions.

This part should not be underestimated as it impacts all else in the pitch deck and business. A founder should be patient here to get the audience to care about the problem as much as the founder does. 21done's problem definition is split up into the introduction of the persona—Millennial Lena—and her problem (see Fig. 3.5).

3. *Solution*: Next, the question is "How is your product going to solve the problem"? Solution presentation needs to match the problem description in a very consistent way. For example if two problems are introduced, the solution should directly address these two problems by showing clearly how these would be solved. The solution is THE

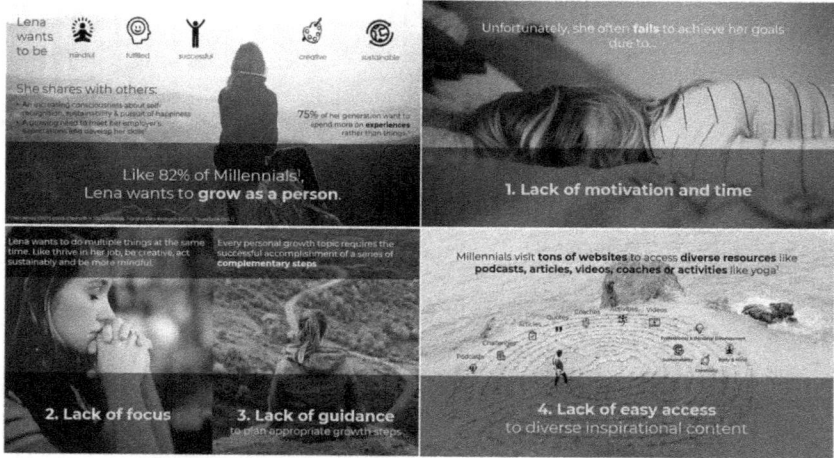

Fig. 3.5 Problem description by 21done

slide that needs to provide credibility to the vision, value proposition statements and USPs. Why should investors trust those statements? Solution is the key here. This implies that the solution should not focus on the status quo of the start-up's product, but on the product vision. It is a good practice to demonstrate how the life of the persona will look like when he uses the solution. Finally, it is important that the solution presentation is lean by, for example focusing on an easy three-step process (see Fig. 3.6).

4. *USP aka Competition*: A solution that matches the problem is a must-have. However, the solution also needs to offer features that none of the competitors can provide. Therefore, a slide is needed to provide a competitor analysis and to showcase the reason why this particular start-up's idea is superior and different. A common way to do so is by putting the key USPs of the start-up in different rows and competitors in multiple columns (see Fig. 3.7). Brief text, harvey balls or other easy means can then provide a quick way to show the difference.

5. *Business Model/Revenue Model*: This is a core slide for investors as they want to know how the return of their investment works. Different revenue models have been shown in Sect. 5.2.1 of this book. The relevant one(s) need to be described (see Fig. 3.8). It is not unlikely that

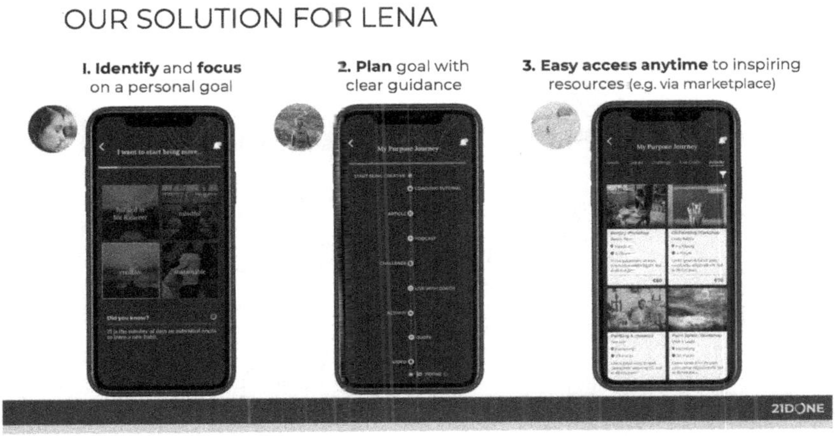

3 Starting a Start-Up 43

OUR SOLUTION FOR LENA

1. Identify and **focus** on a personal goal

2. Plan goal with clear guidance

3. Easy access anytime to inspiring resources (e.g. via marketplace)

Fig. 3.6 Solution description by 21done

#2: STRONG USPs ...   ... FOR B2C   & B2B

	21DONE	B2C competitors	B2B competitors
I. Clear Step-By-Step & Purpose Guidance			
Purpose-driven goals to focus on	●	◐	○
(Ease of) customisation	●	◐	○
Structure & clarity	●	◐	○
II. Strong Motivation to Engage			
Social impact*	●	○	○
Progressive lifestyle brand	●	◐	◐
III. Accessibility of Inspirational Content			
Easy access to holistic set of resources	●	◐	◐
Inspirational power of each resource	◐	◐	◐
IV. Empathic Growth Perspective on Individual (B2B)			
Employees seen as person, not employee	●		◐

* Personal growth activities are seamlessly connected to the support of: 1) Small businesses, 2) Social projects

Fig. 3.7 USP description by 21done

the business model changes with the evolution of the start-up. It may also be planned from the very beginning that after a basic revenue model has been launched, another revenue stream will be added. Especially digital ecosystems like Facebook, Google, or Apple added many new revenue streams after acquiring a fist large user base.

#1: SCALABLE BUSINESS MODEL (FOR B2C & B2B)

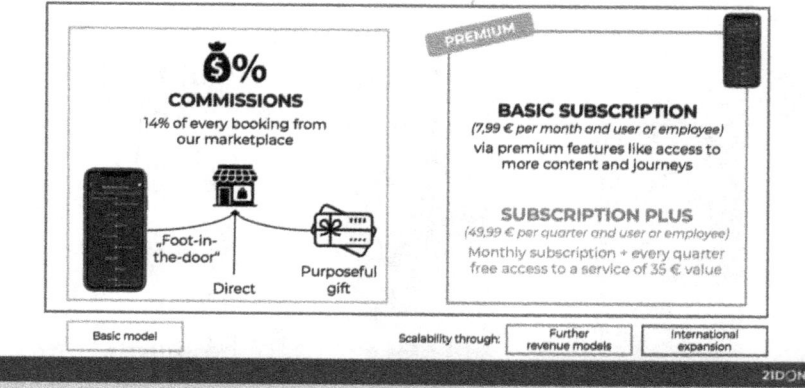

Fig. 3.8 Business model of 21done

6. *Market Size and Opportunity:* Investors want to invest in growing markets that are big enough. A structured analysis of the market size will show the investor that the founder understands the market and its submarkets. In which submarkets is the start-up going to start and why? The point of this slide is to show investors that ideally, there is a large, untapped market for the start-up's product. One approach to show market understanding and market potential is the TAM-SAM-SOM approach (see Fig. 3.9).

TAM refers to the total addressable market. Particularly at the beginning, this market potential is not achievable for start-ups, but also not recommended to target as this would stand in contrast to a focused market approach. SAM refers to the serviceable addressable market. This market seems more appropriate for the start-up to look at because of the specific solution the start-up offers for a more niche market. However, the SAM reflects more the potential the start-up may "grow in". A clear focus for the first start-up phase means that the start-up strives for the SOM—the serviceable obtainable market.

Another common way to express the market opportunity is to show volume and growth rates of the different fields of operation of the start-up. This approach has been taken by 21done (see Fig. 3.10).

TAM SAM SOM

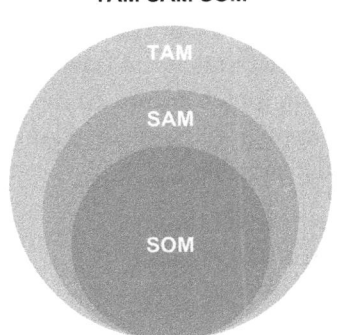

Total Addressable Market
Total Market for a company's product

Serviceable Available Market
Portion of the market a company can acquire based on your business model

Serviceable Obtainable Market
Percentage of SAM a company can realistically capture

Fig. 3.9 The TAM SAM SOM approach (adapted from Chi, 2021)

Fig. 3.10 Market opportunity description by 21done

7. *Go-To-Market*: In the go-to-market slide, the following questions must be answered:
   (a) How are you going to get customers?
   (b) What is the 1-year roadmap for reaching which (revenue) milestones? Milestones can be based on a founder's assumptions on future investor funding.

8. *Traction*: All previous points are rather conceptual. Investors will gain much confidence in the start-up if it shows that there are first paying customers or at least users engage on a frequent basis with the solution. Tangible results will serve as strong proof points. In case of monthly growth, an investor will happily extrapolate figures. Therefore, any data is powerful here. Examples are:

    (a) Hundreds of people are excited about the solution
    (b) People share the start-up's postings on social media
    (c) X customers have been paying y €

9. *Financials:* The revenue model indicated how the company is earning money. Following that, it is important to show how much money is expected over the first 3–5 years. Apart from revenues, further important KPIs like number of customers, CPA or EBIT should be calculated in a business case and summarised in this pitch slide. In the end, the investor wants to know the return he can expect in the long run.

10. *Team:* An evaluation of a start-up at the beginning is rather Art than Science. While more data values such as revenues and number of customers will be available to assess a start-up's price at a later stage, this does not exist early on. Hence, the evaluation is more difficult, and the investor will mainly base his decision on his impression of the team. This is why the team slide is the second most-viewed page in a pitch deck (Hannah, n.d.). Questions to be answered on this slide:

    (a) Who is your team?
    (b) What are they good at?
    (c) Why are they going to help lead the business to success?

It is important to focus on the core experiences and reference of each team member that is very much related to what the start-up is focusing on. Logos to indicate references can be added here. As with all other slides: Less is more. An investor needs to understand the core reason why a team member was recruited to progress the company (Fig. 3.11).

11. *Ask:* A pitch is motivated by a certain goal the founder has in mind. Most of the time, the founder aims to raise capital. Besides stating the exact value, the founder will need to specify the milestones to be

Fig. 3.11 Team description by 21done

Fig. 3.12 Ask description by 21done

achieved within a specific time period (see Fig. 3.12). Milestones can refer to acquiring customers, generating revenue, or launching a product. However, there can also be different motivations for pitching, like convincing a person to join as a co-founder or strategic advisor. A start-up always needs something!

Process of Creating and Presenting a Pitch Deck

It is not advisable to create a pitch deck with the content mentioned above right away. Rather there need to be some preparations that we summarise in the following process steps (adapted from Dirk Lehmann & Partners).

1. *Collect Content*: All slides of a pitch deck need to be researched intensively. For example the problem description should be backed up by data. Collect all content pieces on post-its to think through the pitch story.
2. *Draft the Story*: Take a piece of paper and a pencil and create a matrix as indicated in Fig. 3.13. Every "cell" represents one slide. Put the message of each slide in the title of the slide. All titles together should make the full story of the presentation. Content below the title should represent the title in a visual way. The title itself should serve as the summary then for the full slide. It is also advisable to write the story in a word document. In any case, the design of proper slides should wait until the storyline is validated with experts and consumers. The story should be well understood, ignite excitement, and indicate strong business potential.

Agenda 1. Introduction 2. Analysis 3. Strategy 4. …	…	…
…	…	…
…	…	…

Fig. 3.13 Pitch deck storyline template

3. *Slides Creation:* With adequate positive feedback on the script and story, slides can now be developed. Slides should support the story, not the other way around. A common failure is that it shows much more, which results in irritation and distracts from the core story. Also, the design should be clean, simple, and attractive. It should NOT be overdone, meaning that design should not try to distract from missing logic or substance. Slides should be tested again. Keep in mind to have two versions: one to present and one to send. The latter contains more text as the first.
4. *Rehearse and Memorise*: Memorise your script and presentation to perfection to showcase maximum confidence once you go on stage and be sure that you will mention everything you wanted to in a relaxed manner.
5. *Present*: Be passionate and professional. Be authentic and do not try to make things up or be funny. Nothing wrong with being funny, but do not try when you are not. Be confident. You can increase confidence by large extents when having practiced the pitch at least 20 times.

3.3 Step-by-Step Framework to Create a CX-Centric Start-Up

The earlier chapters have provided a theoretical understanding of the concept of customer experience as well as provided the basics when starting a start-up. With that as a foundation, this chapter will provide an overview of the step-by-step guide to creating a customer experience-centric start-up (see Fig. 3.14), which will be elaborated in Chaps. 4–6.

The first step of the framework, as covered in Chap. 3, provides a start-up package to guide start-ups in identifying the initial problem to fix as well as advice on pitch creation which is a vital ingredient for a start-up's success. Next, the second step focuses on supporting companies to understand customers and their environment. Firstly, companies will be guided to identify their potential customers, define the target group, and understanding them in detail through various frameworks and tools to gather insights for the refinement of the identified customer problem and

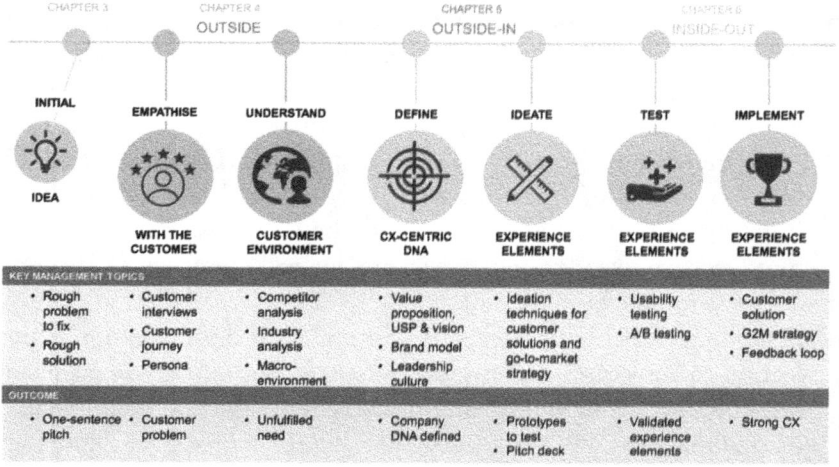

Fig. 3.14 The customer experience framework

solution idea. The third step then provides a framework to assist companies to take a dive into the micro- and macroenvironment of the customers and companies, including tools to support the analysis of the industry, competitors, and general trends, to better inform business strategies. With a well-defined customer problem, solution, and a good understanding of the general environment, step four helps companies synthesise this information to generate the business and brand strategy, which sets the basis of the next step. With a solid business and brand strategy, step five continues to support companies in their move towards the ideation and designing of the experience elements, particularly the customer solution and marketing strategy. Step 6 then proceeds to the testing of the experience elements for validation and refinements. Once the ideas are thoroughly tested and validated, the last step completes with the process of implementation for a smooth and effective integration into the customer journey. The steps of the framework will be highlighted in the following chapters.

References

21done. (2020). *Corporate pitch deck*.

Cayasso, J. (2019). *What is a pitch deck presentation guide template and examples*. Accessed September 25, 2021, from https://slidebean.com/blog/what-is-a-pitch-deck-presentation-meaning

Chi, C. (2021). *TAM SAM SOM: What do they mean & how do you calculate them?* Accessed September 25, 2021, from https://blog.hubspot.com/marketing/tam-sam-som

Founder Institute. (2021a). *How to pitch your startup*. Accessed September 25, 2021, from https://fi.co/pitch_deck

Founder Institute. (2021b). *Startup Madlibs: Perfecting your one sentence pitch*. Accessed November, 2021, from https://fi.co/madlibs

Gilchrist, K. (2020). How a 32-year-old turned a high school yearbook idea into a $3.2 billion business. *CNBC*. Accessed July 10, 2021, from https://www.cnbc.com/2020/01/09/canva-how-melanie-perkins-built-a-3point2-billion-dollar-design-start-up.html

Graham, P. (2012). *How to get startup ideas*. Accessed July 20, 2021, from http://paulgraham.com/startupideas.html

Bill Gurley. (2015). *In defense of the deck*. Accessed July 20, 2021, from http://abovethecrowd.com/2015/07/07/in-defense-of-the-deck/

Hannah, J. (n.d.). *The team slide: You had me at hello*. Accessed September 26, 2021, from https://www.forentrepreneurs.com/team-slide/

Jobs, S. (2007). *D5 Conference*. Accessed July 12, 2021, from https://allaboutstevejobs.com/videos/misc/d5_conference_steve_2007

Lefcourt, J. (2016). *Founders, your goal of VC Meeting №1? Meeting №2*. Accessed September 10, 2021, from https://medium.com/@jennylefcourt/founders-your-goal-of-vc-meeting-1-meeting-2-e420_36c9675

Dirk Lehmann & Partners. (2021). https://dirk-lehmann.com/

Ressi, A. (n.d.). *Startup Madlibs: Perfecting your one sentence pitch*. Accessed July 20, 2021, from https://fi.co/madlibs

4

Understanding the Outside World: Customers and the Surrounding Environment

All corporate concepts and services aimed at the market must have a common starting point: the customer, or more precisely, the (desired) customer experience. This chapter provides a guide for companies to deepen their understanding of customers as well as the surrounding environment, which can have a significant impact on their perceptions, attitudes, and behaviour.

4.1 Customer Analysis

According to Kahneman and Lovallo (1993), entrepreneurs are often prone to optimism bias and hold an overly optimistic perception of the success of their business. They can also often be overwhelmed by the excitement of their solution that they overlook the need to validate their idea with the end customers. Many interesting businesses do not end up far as they do not serve any market needs. As such, the importance of customer understanding and idea validation cannot be undermined.

4.1.1 Defining Customer Personas

Consumers are individuals with unique characteristics, lifestyle, values, and needs, which implies that they react differently to various products and marketing. Many companies are concerned about defining target groups due to the fear of excluding potential consumers. In fact, on a contrary, targeting enables companies to focus their limited budget and brand offerings on a specific market that is most likely to purchase (Porta, 2021).

The first step to creating a target persona is to identify the segment(s) which the company would like to target. A well-defined target group provides companies with information that simplifies the decisions as to where and how the company should market. The following steps provide a guide to creating a clear target group. In the process of defining the target group, it is also important to keep in mind the eventual market size, the ability of the company to reach the target group with its existing capabilities and the purchasing power (Fig. 4.1).

Firstly, the base of the target group can be defined as consumers who resonate with the rough customer problem identified at the beginning. Following that, the persona can be built with more characteristics with the following:

Demographics Demographic segmentation is one of the most used bases as consumer needs and desires are closely related to demographic variables and are often easier to measure. Demographic variables include

Segmentation Variable	Examples
Geographic	Continents, countries, regions, states, provinces, population density, neighbourhoods, climate
Demographic	Age, life-cycle stage, gender, income, occupation, education, religion, ethnicity, generation, marital status
Psychographic	Social class, lifestyle, personality
Behavioural	Occasions, benefits, user status, usage rate, loyalty

Fig. 4.1 Overview of segmentation variables (adapted from Kotler & Armstrong, 2014)

factors such as age, life-cycle stage, gender, income, occupation, education, religion, ethnicity, and generation (Kotler & Armstrong, 2014). The company should determine the variables which are of relevance, particularly those which have a strong relation to the customer problem identified.

Geographic Geographic variables include factors such as countries, states, regions, and cities (Kotler & Armstrong, 2014). Geographical segmentation can be crucial as socio-cultural context can vary significantly across the different geographical units, which may also give rise to different needs and expectations. Companies should keep in mind the adaptations required to target certain geographic variables such as language, legal regulations, and currency when deciding which geographic variables are important.

Psychographics Defining the target group with psychographics variables is crucial as people in the same geographic and demographic groups can vary largely in this aspect. Increasingly, purchase decisions are driven by values and lifestyles, as such, psychographic characteristics, including personality, attitudes, values, motives, interests, and lifestyles, provide a more specific view of the customers to inform business decisions and inch the business closer to the right customers who are willing to purchase. Here, the limbic map in Sect. 4.1.2 can also be used to provide a psychographic classification for the target customers.

Behavioural Taking behavioural bases such as knowledge, attitudes, uses, and product-related responses, including benefits, loyalty, and usage rate (Kotler & Armstrong, 2014) into consideration when defining the target group is particularly important as it provides knowledge on how the customer interacts with the brand and their actual actions, which can supply the company with real knowledge about consumers that can be used to move them down the funnel. In fact, many companies overlook the importance of psychographic and behavioural variables, which are extremely essential to creating strong customer experience, as they provide further insights into customer emotions and underlying motives and actual behaviour information, instead of assumptions based on demogra-

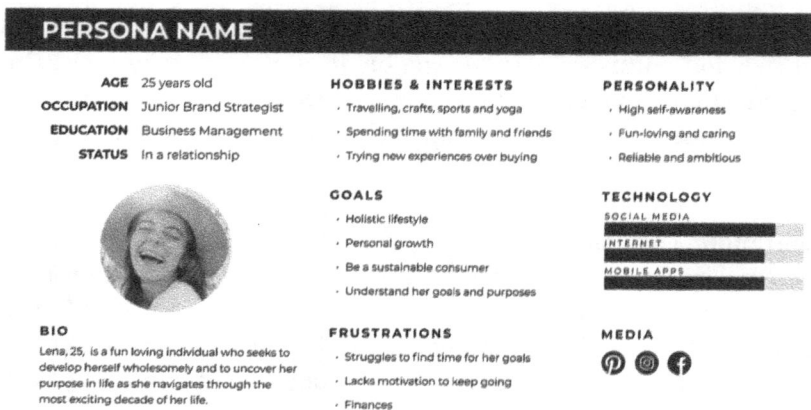

Fig. 4.2 Customer persona template with example

phy and geographic. This information can significantly support the customer journey mapping, which is key to creating strong CX. Once the target group has been defined, companies can then move on to creating their target persona as it will serve as the centrepiece for deeper customer understanding. Customer personas are "fictional characters created to represent a target group or audience with its different user (arche)types, which are built around observed behaviour patterns among real people. Each persona is representative of a segment of the target group" (Brunello, 2018). Customer personas are created to allow businesses to better understand their lead customers to inform marketing and communication strategies. They include comprehensive information about the target group, e.g. demographics, psychographics, goals, frustrations, skills, behaviour, and personality (see Fig. 4.2).

To create accurate representations of target customers, it is important to obtain facts and information of real customers through analytics data such as purchase behaviour and other research methods instead of basing solely on company assumptions. Companies that do not yet have real customers can leverage on information from potential customers identified from initial interviews conducted to validate the customer problem. By collecting these data, the company can construct a more human character that goes beyond basic demographics to also include emotive information, which plays a more important role in determining their purchase decisions (Brunello, 2018).

It is important to keep in mind that a persona is not something set in stone but requires regular revisits and refinement with new data collected. In the following chapter, frameworks which support companies to better understand their customers will be introduced. With increasing knowledge of the target customers, companies should continually refine their defined persona to have an up-to-date reflection of the target customer. This iterative process of understanding and refining is important in helping the company align its strategy to provide fit for its customers. In addition, while there is no limit to the number of personas a company or brand can create, it is recommended for start-ups to start and focus on one or two in order to achieve a good depth of analysis and targeting to validate its business idea and gain traction in view of its limited resources.

4.1.2 Uncovering Underlying Customer Needs

"The more we understand the consumer, the more we understand the essence of customer experience. The more we understand customer experience, the more we can shape it, develop it, and better service the customer" (Newman & McClimans, 2019). Beyond understanding how customers act, it is often of more strategic value to uncover the why behind their actions. The following chapters provide practical tools to help companies gain a deeper understanding of their customers to refine their initial idea as well as to better inform other business and strategic decisions.

Empathy Map
You cannot understand someone until you have walked a mile in their shoes. The Empathy Map (see Fig. 4.3), a framework that provides different user perspective areas a company should study to gain deeper customer insights, can be used to understand underlying emotions and values. The Empathy Map also encompasses the concept of jobs-to-be-done (see point 2). Harvard Business School marketing professor Theodore Levitt said "People don't want to buy a quarter-inch drill. They want a quarter-inch hole"! (Christensen & Raynor, 2003). By understanding the "why", the company can then innovate to offer a solution to help consumers

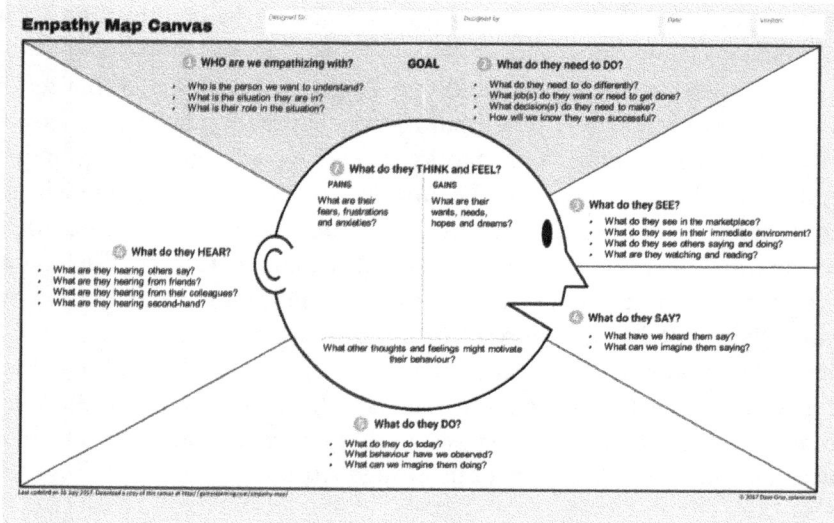

Fig. 4.3 Empathy map canvas (Gray, 2017)

accomplish their jobs better, quicker, or cheaper, one that customers are more than willing to pay for (Ulwick, 2016).

In order to employ this framework effectively, the following five steps should be followed. Firstly, the subject and scope which the company is interested in understanding should be determined. In this case, the customer persona and problem defined in the earlier chapter can serve as the input. Secondly, user data, general and empathy map-specific, should be gathered through primary and secondary research. As mentioned, actual user information instead of presumptions should be used whenever possible as it is more accurate and informative. Thirdly, empathy mapping is best executed with a team as every individual brings his unique perspective to the table, making the outcome more objective. To prepare for the collaboration, the appropriate materials such as sticky notes and writing materials, or even a digital collaborative canvas tool such as Miro or Mural can be set up. Fourthly, the information gathered in step two should be read and reviewed by all participants. Lastly, the team should gather to contribute their individual input to the empathy map by translating the customer information into the relevant chapters on the template and synthesise the information by clustering similar ideas (Gibbons, 2019).

By systematically addressing the questions and topics depicted in Fig. 4.3, the aim is to successively advance to the central core of the model: What is the core customer need or desired customer experience and from which non-intuitive customer insight can it be derived? For example the Old Spice brand has used the insight that every man is deeply insecure about his masculinity in its marketing campaigns to address the need for a masculine scent or the desire for a masculine (sensory) experience. Eventually, the outcome of the empathy map serves to provide a comprehensive visualisation of the target customer and can be easily handed to different stakeholders for a common understanding of the target customers.

Limbic Map

The Limbic Map by Häusel (2019) was created on the basis that human decisions are largely driven by emotions. This means that businesses need to develop an understanding of consumer emotional needs in order to align their strategies and communication with that of the potential customers (Rehfeld, 2019). The map (see Fig. 4.4) visually represents the result of extensive scientific findings in the fields of neurology,

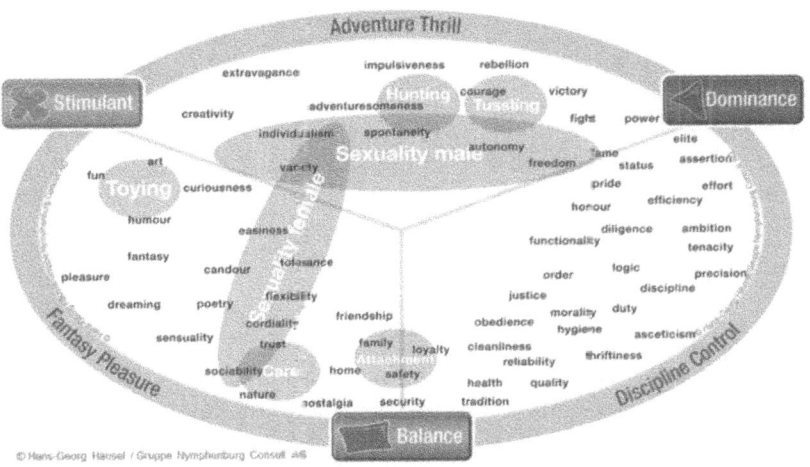

Fig. 4.4 The limbic map (Häusel, 2011)

psychology, sociology, and philosophy, and captures central motive and emotional systems which guide people's actions and behaviours (Häusel, 2019).

The motive and emotion systems depicted on the map are predisposed in every human being but to varying degrees. Based on the Limbic Map, three central emotion and motive systems can be identified: Dominance, Stimulant, and Balance. The balance system relates to the pursuit of security and certainty, the stimulant system relates to the pursuit of creativity and fun, while the dominance system relates to the need for power and control. Since no individual fits perfectly into one of these areas, "intermediate areas", which result from the combination of two of the three superordinate systems, can also be defined. The combination of dominance and stimulant results in adventurousness. The combination of dominance and balance results in control, and that of balance and stimulant results in fantasy. In general, there are seven different Limbic types (Häusel, 2011):

- Harmoniser: High level of social and family orientation; low ascendancy and status orientation; desire for security
- Open-minded: Open to new things, sense of well-being, tolerance, mild pleasure
- Hedonist: Active search for new things, high level of individualism and spontaneity
- Adventurer: Risk taker, low impulse control
- Performer: High level of performance and status orientation, ambitious
- Disciplinarian: High sense of responsibility and details, low desire for consumption
- Traditionalist: Low level of future orientation, desire for order and security

Companies can use the limbic map to identify the limbic type(s) of their target customers and use this knowledge to guide its brand and communication strategy. The limbic map is more suitable for a deeper understanding of the target group's general emotional needs and motives which can provide insights into the customer problem. This can be used after analysing the initial customer problem and behaviour, which is also helpful for the design of product and communication strategies. For example IKEA's target group which consists of middle-class young couples or families with young children who want to be creative in their home furnishing but not spend excessively fall somewhere between the stimulation and balance systems (Harmoniser and open-minded types) (Rehfeld, 2019). To align with that, IKEA's showrooming strategy provides novel and family-oriented interior ideas to stimulate imagination and motivate them to try something new for their homes.

Five Whys

The five-whys technique, also known as the root cause analysis or laddering, is another tool that can be employed to uncover the source of a customer problem, from questioning the customer behaviour to revealing the underlying motive. Unearthing the source is the basis for understanding the core of a problem which can then give rise to solutions targeted at the root. Firstly, an initial customer problem should be identified. Following that, a series of "whys" should be repeatedly asked, after each response, to drill down to the real root cause (see Fig. 4.5).

The process should only cease when no further "why" can be asked. However, it is important to be sensitive to the situation and avoid cause irritation to participants by making the interview come across as an

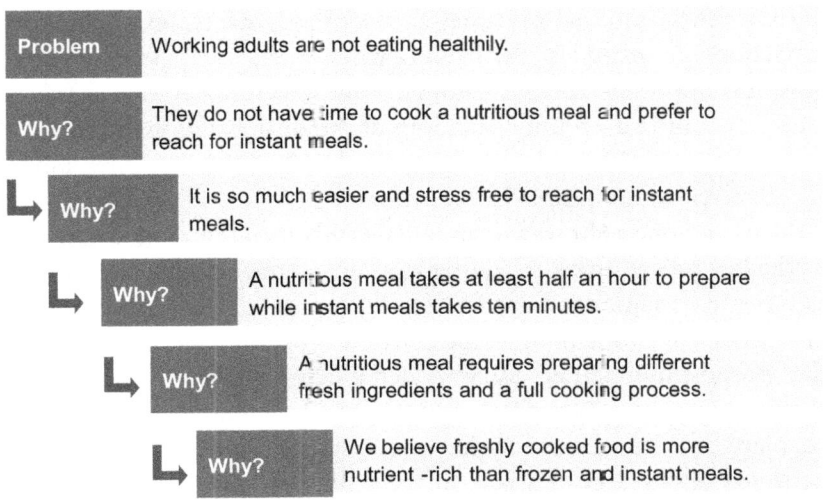

Fig. 4.5 The five why technique, also known as laddering

interrogation (Interaction Design Foundation, 2016). With the different levels of the problem identified, the company can then ideate around it.

Customer Journey Map

A customer journey map is a visual representation of *customer interactions and touchpoints* with an organisation from the *customer's point of view*, which includes the *customer experiences* in pre-purchase, purchase, and post-purchase stages such as positive and negative thoughts, emotions, motives, and attitudes, and identifies the moments of truth including pain and gain points in the relationship between the customers and the organisation and identifies improvement opportunities for the organisation (Lemon & Verhoef, 2016).

CX is "the customer's overall perception of a brand including cognitive, emotional, physical, sensorial, spiritual, and social responses to interactions throughout the customer journey which brings about significant impact on business performance" helps to recall that CX is created over time and in different phases of the user journey.

To understand a customer journey, companies need to create a journey map that captures the customer's experience from pre-purchase to post-purchase. Many companies today continue to use a simplified customer journey map focusing on touchpoints, which is behaviour-centric and does not reflect internal processes such as thoughts, feelings, emotions, motivations, or attitudes. Particularly when managing customer experiences, it is important to have a human-centred approach such that companies can gain a deep understanding of the business problem from the customer perspective to deliver features which are value-adding and fitting to the customer profile (Stegemann, 2021).

There is no one right way to visualise a customer-centred journey map, but the key to a truly value-adding map lies in the breadth and depth of customer information it captures. The customer journey map in Fig. 4.6 is a synthesis of a touchpoint-based customer journey, empathy map and value proposition canvas that provides a comprehensive framework to achieve a deep understanding of not only where customer interactions take place but also customer behaviour, responses, internal processes and uncovered opportunities based on the pain and gain points identified. The outcome of the journey map is extremely crucial for companies as it identifies the touchpoints to be managed and optimised, and provides

4 Understanding the Outside World: Customers...

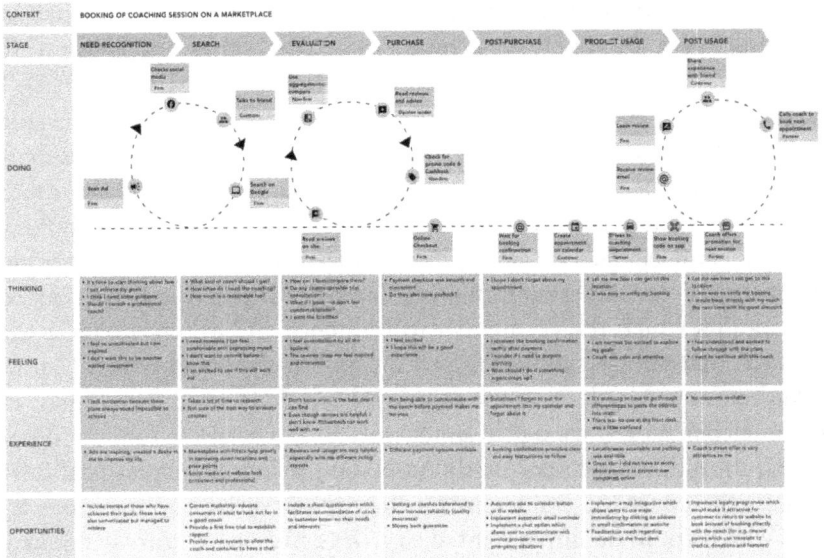

Fig. 4.6 Customer journey mapping with example (adapted from Risdon, 2012)

the basis for ideation of experience elements (Sect. 5.3.3). In most cases, companies need to create two customer journey maps; the first map to reflect the current customer journey and the second to illustrate the difference due to the company's innovation. Especially for start-ups, the first map will focus on customer journey with potential competitors, which is important for the identification of gaps to fill, and the second map will reflect the new journey of customers with the start-up and its touchpoints (Stegemann, 2021).

How should companies begin to create this map? Firstly, companies should define their customer persona as the entire customer journey is centred around the persona. In this case, the persona defined in the earlier chapter should be used. While it is recommended to focus on a single persona for each journey, there could be situations where a multiple-persona journey map makes sense. For instance, the company could have multiple personas who are very different in their needs but are embarking on a similar journey. In such a case, combining both on a single journey map may help to identify opportunities that add value to both personas. Mapping them separately may result in opportunities and ideas which create gain for one but increase pain for the other (Schebrova, 2018). In the context of a young start-up, a single persona journey is recommended such that focus can be placed on the target persona to ensure an in-depth understanding as well as effective resource usage. Secondly, the touchpoints and channels where relevant interactions take place should be identified and categorised into different stages, mostly related to the customer funnel. In addition, it may also be helpful to distinguish between touchpoints which the company can influence and others which it cannot such that efforts can be focused on the former touchpoints (Lemon & Verhoef, 2016). Next, at the respective touchpoints and channels, the customer behaviour, thoughts, emotions, and experience (gain and pain points) should be captured. Lastly, based on the first three points of information, the company can begin to identify potential opportunities and ideas which could be implemented to relieve their pain points and create gains for them.

According to McKinsey research (2017), customers experience and interact with companies through end-to-end experiences, not touchpoints, and that overall experience can still be poor even if individual touchpoints are well managed. As such, it is important to note that while touchpoint management is crucial, it is also important to take a zoomed-out perspective to analyse how successive touchpoints interrelate (De Keyser et al., 2015) and how experiences from one touchpoint to another is seamless. By adopting a customer journey perspective, companies are more likely to deliver a strong and holistic customer experience.

Data Collection Method

The preceding chapters may have raised the question: where exactly can this customer information be obtained from? Fortunately, in this data-driven era, consumer information can be easily accessed from secondary sources, and new data can be created through conducting primary research (see Fig. 4.7). The specific number and type of sources should be determined in each individual case based on the criteria of time, cost, and added value.

For most start-ups, the initial focus would be on company-owned data such as business and customer records as well as publicly available

4 Understanding the Outside World: Customers... 65

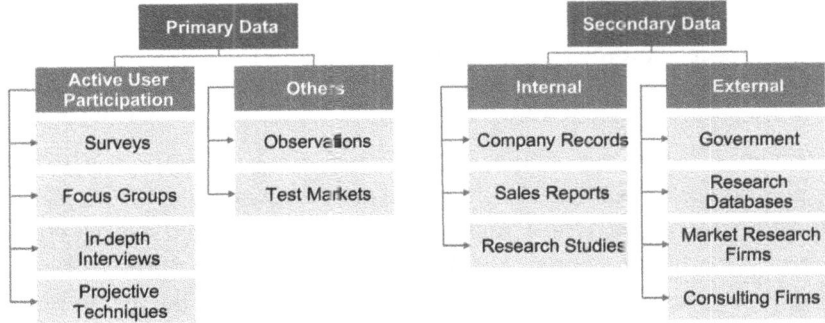

Fig. 4.7 Overview of research methods and data sources (adapted from Sarstedt & Mooi, 2019)

Primary Research	Description	Use Case
Interviews	• One-to-one Interactive session with participants about a particular topic • Unstructured, semi-structured or structured • Allows for probing for deeper understanding or clarification • Quantitative and qualitative	To gain in-depth understanding of customer needs and motives To identify significant variables which can be later tested in a focus group or surveys
Surveys	• Questionnaire posted to participants who have to answer the questions • Contains different questions types including multiple choice, checkboxes, open-ended and scales • Quantitative and qualitative	Understanding significant consumer perspectives on various factors
Focus Group	• Interviews conducted with 4 to 6 participants at the same time • Facilitated by a moderator • 60 to 120 minutes • Qualitative	Makes inferences on respondents' attitudes, feelings, beliefs, experiences and reactions
Ethnography	• Observations are performed in the natural state of the participants • Researcher participates and settles in the background • Behaviour is usually recorded • Qualitative	Understanding actual consumer behaviours which may be sub-conscious

Fig. 4.8 Overview of primary research methods

information, as accessing detailed customer and industry reports can be costly. However, depending on the specificity of the customer problem the company is exploring, it can be difficult to find relevant data. In such cases, primary research methods could add value by creating new knowledge for specific customer problem investigations.

Primary research can be executed with various methods, as seen in Fig. 4.8. In this chapter, the most common techniques, including interviews, surveys, focus groups and ethnography, will be further elaborated on. Every research method has its own advantages and limitations, and companies can employ a combination of methods to supplement the data collection process.

Interviews Interviews are qualitative one-to-one conversations with participants about a particular subject (Sarstedt & Mooi, 2019). Interviews can be unstructured, semi-structured, or highly structured. Unstructured interviews are highly suitable if the objective is to collect initial insights about a topic as the interviewer is able to pose questions flexibly in return to the interviewee's responses, allowing the conversation to flow freely and expand in various directions. On the other hand, highly structured interviews follow a fixed questioning sequence and do not allow for flexibility. These are used if the research objective is to fairly evaluate responses across the same bases. In most cases, companies use semi-structured interviewers where a sequence of questions has been prepared in advance, but interviews have the flexibility to probe and include additional questions to gain a deeper understanding to a topic. This allows for a structured yet spontaneous approach which is highly suitable in the context of gaining an in-depth understanding of consumers at the beginning.

Surveys Surveys are the most used primary research method where information about respondents' knowledge, attitudes, preferences, and purchase behaviour is collected (Kotler & Armstrong, 2014). Surveys can be conducted in person, by mail or remotely, which allows for high levels of flexibility. In general, surveys include a questionnaire that can take on many different question types such as multiple-choice, checkboxes, open-ended, and scales, depending on the research objective and whether quantitative or qualitative data is required. To run an effective survey research, there are various aspects to take into consideration, including the sample size, question types, survey flow, question construction and more, which should be further explored if desired. While surveys typically do not support probing and in-depth questioning, they are the most time-efficient and cost-effective (when conducted on a large scale) to achieve a general understanding of bigger sample size, which is more accurate and telling than a few interviews.

Focus Groups Another popular qualitative and exploratory research method is focus groups. Focus groups are interviews conducted among 4–6 participants in one setting and facilitated by a moderator (Sarstedt & Mooi, 2019). Focus groups are usually carried out to collect in-depth insights about a community's perception and opinions on a subject, e.g. new ideas, products, and purchase behaviour. In addition, participants of a focus group are usually determined based on a set of specific criteria such as demography, which is dependent on the purpose of the research. During a focus group, participants are allowed to discuss and bounce off each other's ideas and comments as these conversations can give rise to more complex and detailed insights. Focus groups are usually held for a duration of 60–120 min, depending on the number of participants and the flow of the discussion. The focus group moderator plays a crucial role in the success of the research process as he needs to ensure that all participants have the opportunity to speak, express their opinions and that the discussion stays on topic (Kotler & Armstrong, 2014).

Ethnography Actions speak louder than words. While surveys and interviews help to collect useful consumer information, the data collected may be incomplete as customers may not be conscious of their actual behaviour or deliberately withhold certain information, i.e. people may say they do something but in reality, do something completely different. As such, ethnographic research can be conducted to gather complementary insights, which can provide the company a competitive edge over its competitors as this information is more difficult to uncover and mostly overlooked (Dalton, 2017). Ethnographic research is becoming increasingly employed in the realm of marketing and consumer understanding, especially in product and service designs related to improving the lives of people. This type of research is conducted to help companies understand the things that people say and do, their feelings and the objects they use, how they use them and the motivation behind their behaviour, emotions, and speech (Venkatesh et al., 2017).

The scope of the ethnographic research should be based on the customer problem identified. One of the main principles for conducting such research is naturalism. Since the aim is to capture naturally occurring human behaviour in real world context, the research should be carried out wherever the behaviour commonly occurs and in contexts that are relevant to the customer problem (Venkatesh et al., 2017). During the research, the researcher is expected to note down the observations and record with tools such as voice recorders and cameras. The duration of an ethnographic research can take from hours to days and varies with the sample size as well as the research objective (Stickdorn et al., 2018). However, it is important to recognise that additional time allowance should be provided for the development of rapport between the researcher and participants and for the interviewer to gradually vanish into the natural environment of the participant such that naturalistic consumer behaviour can emerge. During the research, the researchers are also expected to hold discussions with the participants whenever a deeper understanding of a particular behaviour or perspective is required (Estey, 2019). In general, ethnography is useful for investigating the real behaviour of consumers to understand how products and services can be designed to support or solve their problems. However, ethnography is time-consuming and costly and requires a trained researcher to execute the research process.

For instance, Miele, a German household appliance manufacturer, conducted ethnographic research to observe the cleaning practice of families with children who have allergies. Miele deployed "listen and watch" teams for the home visits and found out that these parents vacuumed a mattress multiple times a day to ensure that it is clean. However, they did not lament about the additional amount of time and cleaning intensity required because it became part of the routine, and they were used to it. Through this, the team realised the strong need to develop a vacuum cleaner that can detect if a surface that was cleaned is dust-free or not. As such, Miele integrated a hygiene sensor into their vacuum cleaner, which turned from red to amber to green to indicate the dust presence, which became a breakthrough feature for families with allergies as they could always check for the need to clean with the sensor and not have to clean it several times because they could not know if the surface is truly dust-free or not (Goffin et al., 2012). This is a clear example showcasing the strength of ethnographic research in uncovering underlying needs by going beyond spoken insights to observe and unravel sub-conscious behaviour.

Social Listening Another important source of customer understanding which should not be overlooked is social media. The world sees over 3.6 billion social media users, and the number is projected to increase to 4.4 billion in 2025 (Statista, 2020). The key is, customers are not only using social media for entertainment purposes but also as an outlet for expressing their opinions about their daily life, their desires and their problems. Customer understanding is at the heart of customer experience-centric organisations, and social listening helps companies hear what their customers or potential customers think, feel, and experience, giving insights into existing and future opportunities, which are valuable knowledge for creating strong customer experiences. Social listening is the process of analysing conversations and trends to uncover insights about brands, products, industry, and competitors to help companies make more informed strategic decisions (Clark, 2020).

For the purpose of new product development, social listening can add value by identifying pain points that customers have with existing solutions and gain points that lead to customer satisfaction. Based on these insights, companies can ideate and create innovative products which closely fit the market needs. On the other hand, for the purpose of understanding brand perceptions, social listening can also help to identify customer experiences which allow companies to validate if their strategies have been effective and how they can optimise and improve to align customer brand perceptions with their brand identity.

At this point, if necessary, the insights gathered from the chapter should facilitate the refinement of the customer problem statement to better reflect the customer needs. It is important to note that building a customer experience-centric organisation involves putting customers at the centre of the process, which means that companies should largely involve customer perspectives and less of the company's personal assumptions and perceptions.

4.1.3 Customer Problem Validation

It is not sufficient creating a product you think your customers might need; you have to be sure that they definitely need it. In 2013, Facebook collaborated with HTC to produce a smartphone designed with a Facebook home screen. The usual home screen which contains all mobile apps were replaced by an automatically updating Facebook feed, which seemed like an interesting and convenient idea as Facebook was a trending social media platform. Eventually, the product ended up as a flop as Facebook is not the primary use of most smartphone users. Had Facebook done a thorough customer problem validation, they would have avoided the losses for developing a smartphone that was never needed (Booker, 2017).

Hence, it is important to validate the customer problem identified from the analysis performed in the earlier chapter. "Talk to your customers", they say, "because that's the only way to build something people want" (Kahl, 2020). With the initial customer problem identified, it is important to then conduct multiple rounds of interviews with customers who exhibit traits similar to your customer persona to understand the relevance and validity of the problem amongst different customers. For customer problem validation, in-depth qualitative interviews are recommended as it allows for probing to uncover further underlying thoughts, needs, and values.

For these interviews, it is crucial to avoid introducing the business idea but to understand the customer perspective of the identified problem, how they currently solve the problem and how they would ideally solve the problem. The following is a questionnaire template (Wilcox, 2017) to guide the conversation:

- "Tell me about a time you experienced (the identified problem)".
- "What is the hardest part about the (identified problem)"?
- "Why was it that hard"?
- "What have you done to solve the problem"?
- "What is not ideal about the way you have tried to solve the problem"?

During the interviews, listening to the customer is key. While the template serves an interview guide, questions which should be asked are non-exhaustive and interviewer should be flexible enough to react accordingly with follow up questions or to end the interview if he senses that the interviewee shows no interests in the customer problem. It may also be helpful to observe if there are any commonalities amongst your identified lead customers as this could provide insights for refinement of customer persona.

After each round of interview, it is important to refine the customer problem based on the insights gathered and to repeat the process for a few rounds, until the customer problem is clear and strongly echoed by the potential customers. The interviewees selected for the subsequent rounds of interview should also increasingly resemble the identified lead customers in order to arrive at a highly relevant customer problem.

4.2 Environment Analysis

Consumers function in a bigger environment which involve many stakeholders, including companies, industries, the physical environment and so on. Understanding the customer and company's environment is crucial as the actions of these stakeholders can have significant influence on consumer behaviour.

While the previous section focuses on a better understanding of potential future customers, this section outlines concepts to analyse the market environment. Analysing the market environment is an ongoing process for existing companies, no matter of its size. Of course, it is crucial for start-ups, too. It helps founders to find their market positioning, to anticipate potentials and challenges and get inspirations to generate and validate ideas on different levels. Especially the latter aspect is different compared to large companies because start-ups need to create—among others—a completely new business model, company strategy, product, and marketing approach. While established companies already went through various processes of ideation and validation, start-ups need to get a good grasp of what may work in the market.

Kotler and Armstrong (2020) define a company's market environment as actors and forces outside operative marketing activities that affect a company's ability to build and maintain successful relationships with target customers. This means that relationships with customers are at the centre of all marketing efforts. However, successful customer relationships are not solely in the company's control but are influenced by external factors.

It is common to differentiate between micro- and macroenvironmental factors. The microenvironment of a company includes actors that are close to the company and thus directly affect its success in a positive or negative way. The macroenvironment consists of broader, societal forces that are outside of the companies influence but may shape opportunities or pose threats to the company (Kotler & Armstrong, 2020). In the following sub-chapters, the various forces in the micro- and macroenvironment of a company or start-up will be discussed.

4.2.1 The Microenvironment

A well-known and widely used framework that covers most of the forces that experts allocate to the microenvironment is provided by Michael Porter (1979, 2008). He points out five forces that are most important to analyse industries.

In the following sections, the five most important forces, according to Porter, will be discussed and illustrated through an e-bike industry example in Europe. As seen in Fig. 4.9, the five forces include actors along the value chain (suppliers, competitors, and buyers), potential new competitors and substitute products. The original purpose of Porter's framework was to determine the attractiveness of an industry. For a start-up company, it is well suited to analyse (or validate), which opportunities and threats a new company will face when entering an existing industry.

Competition
Competitors are a very important force in the microenvironment of any company. Their positioning and behaviour directly affect the own company's performance and its strategic options. Before analysing

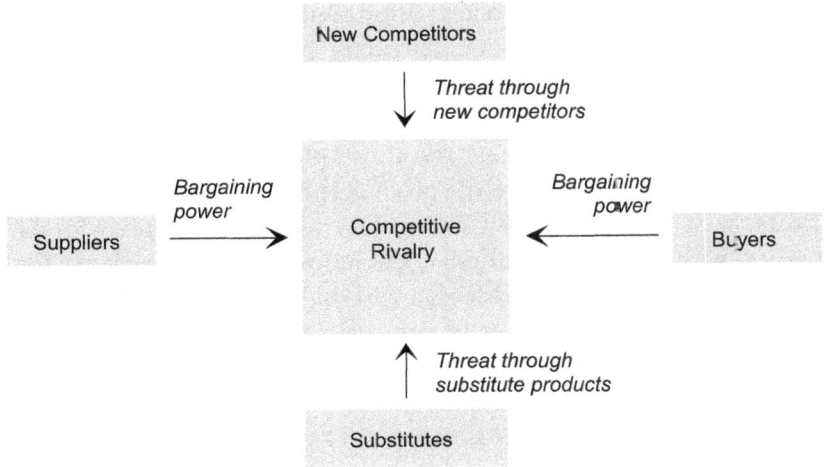

Fig. 4.9 Porter's five forces framework to analyse important aspects of the micro-environment (adapted from Porter, 1979)

competitors, start-ups need to define the industry they target. This may sound simple but is complex in real life and will be illustrated in the following e-bike example.

After defining the market, Porter's framework requires to assess the level of rivalry within the industry. The more rivalry among the firms, the less attractive is the market. The level of rivalry depends on several factors such as:

1. The number of competitors and their market power.
2. The market growth. High market growth typically means less saturated markets and thus to less competitive and less aggressive strategies among the existing firms. Stagnating and shrinking market developments lead to more rivalry.
3. Possibilities for differentiation: homogenous products lead to more rivalry, i.e. price wars. The easier it is to differentiate for companies within the market, the lower the level of rivalry.

This concept will be applied to a rather new company called Cowboy, which produces e-bikes in Europe. The relevant market can be defined in a product-oriented way as "e-bikes within Germany".[1] There are plenty of competitors as most bike manufacturers provide e-bikes nowadays. However, the market is also growing tremendously. The pandemic boosted e-bike sales all over the world in 2020. Experts expect a growing number of potential consumers and thus a stable market growth in the upcoming years. Additionally, the product is not homogenous and offers different ways to differentiate. Cowboy focuses on sporty e-bikes for daily city trips, with a minimalistic design and innovative digital services. Only few competitors, such as VanMoof, are having a similar position and target group. Taking the number of competitors, the market growth, and the differentiation possibilities into account, there currently is a moderate level of rivalry within the industry. However, this is just the status quo and may not hold true for the future.

Suppliers and Collaborators

Many companies depend on suppliers. The more bargaining power suppliers have, the less attractive a market is. A high bargaining power of suppliers is negative as it increases the risk for higher purchase prices. In a market with volatile raw material prices, a supplier with high bargaining power can pass on price fluctuations quite easily. This may jeopardise the profitability of less powerful companies along the value chain.

Bargaining power is typically high if

1. There are only few suppliers in the market.
2. These suppliers are large companies.
3. Switching costs for buyers are high.

In addition to Porter's focus on bargaining power we recommend considering *opportunities* regarding suppliers, too. It may be possible to establish joint ventures or intensive collaborations with suppliers, e.g. by exchanging know-how, technology, or distribution resources. Modern marketing is characterised by a holistic market view that takes all

---

[1] Generally, it is recommended to have demand-oriented market definitions such as "mobility for short and medium distances". However, at this point, it is better to keep it simple and take a product-centered view such as "e-bikes".

stakeholders (including suppliers) into account. Strong partnerships with one or several suppliers can be a competitive advantage.

The term "collaborators" should also be added to Porter's approach. Nowadays, companies should not only analyse the classic product suppliers, but also the many service providers who can add value to the company. For example many start-ups have added value by creating IT interfaces with other products or services. In addition, content partners, (web) designers and other players should also be taken into consideration.

For a company like Cowboy, it is important to know how many suppliers are capable to produce and deliver single parts of their e-bikes. Worldwide, there are many potential suppliers for most parts of e-bikes, even for battery cells. However, the design requirements must be met, and Cowboy is not yet a big player in the market with high sales volumes. Thus, their degree of dependence is rather high. A supplier change is possible, but complex for some parts of the bike, such as the battery. It would certainly disturb production and sales. Due to the growing demand for e-bikes and the pandemic restrictions, there have been extensive supply chain problems for months. A good and stable relationship with suppliers is key in these times.

Buyers

Customers are the most important actors in the microenvironment (Kotler & Armstrong, 2020). The primary aim of modern marketing is to create strong customer relationships and to serve target customers in a way that creates value for both customers and the company. When considering buyers, it is important to have in mind end-users as well as intermediaries.

A market becomes less attractive for (new) companies if buyers

1. Have low switching costs.
2. Show behaviours such as high price sensitivity or low loyalty.
3. Have a decreasing demand in new or existing products.
4. Can play companies off against each other.

This section will not go into detail regarding customers as this book covers the target group explanation in Sect. 4.1.1. For the e-bike industry in Germany, there is a high demand among end-users, which leads to relatively low bargaining power of the customers. That is why price wars are not likely to happen in the near future. This may change once the demand curve flattens as then, end-users have low switching costs and thus more bargaining power. Another "type of end-user" are companies who provide e-bikes to their employees. Their bargaining power is much higher and may force Cowboy to compete in tenders. Other intermediaries are not considered here as Cowboy focuses on direct selling for now.

New Competitors
The vertical axis in the five forces framework represents forces that may have a huge impact on the industry in the future. New competitors can fundamentally change industry dynamics. In some markets, it is likely that new competitors will enter, and in other markets, it is less likely. Factors that increase the likelihood of new competitors are

1. High market growth
2. Low barriers to entry (e. g. capital requirements, distribution channels, economies of scale)
3. Less specific know-how (or if it can easily be acquired)

For the e-bike industry in Germany, many companies have existing resources to build e-bikes. The sporty and smart e-bikes of Cowboy can be easily copied by other established bike manufacturers. However, for new start-ups without any prior heritage in the bike business, the entry barriers are rather high. They would have to build up different supplier relationships, service offerings (such as maintenance and insurance services) and technical know-how in order to be able to sell smart e-bikes for a similar target group. Thus, the main threat for Cowboy are existing bike manufacturers who may be moving towards a similar target group with similar bikes via an already established brand or via a new brand. For Cowboy, it means that rapid growth, exclusive partnerships, and a strong brand are important in order to increase the entry barriers for potential competitors.

Substitutes

A typical mistake in marketing is to define the relevant market too narrowly. Kotler and Armstrong (2020) name it "marketing myopia". Porter's framework accounts for this, with substitute products as fifth force of an industry analysis. The threat from substitute products for an industry depends on factors such as price, quality, and switching costs. Obvious substitutes for butter could be margarine or cream cheese. It is also important to take technological progress into account. What substitute products might be developed in the future?

What are potential substitute products for an e-bike manufacturer such as Cowboy? Firstly, it is important for start-ups to broaden their scope and understand the relevant market as "demand for mobility in urban areas". With this, it becomes clearer that e-scooter, public transportation and (e-)cars are potential substitute products. For example if prices for e-scooters are getting cheaper, or if the government improves public transportation regarding price or quality, Cowboy's business is likely to be affected. Additionally, it is crucial to consider shared service offering for cars, bikes, and e-scooters as potential threat. Shared services providers have spread in recent years, too. A proper analysis should be more detailed and investigate each substitute product on dimensions such as price, convenience, and other motives (e. g. independence and security).

Porter's five forces framework does not cover every aspect of the microenvironment. Kotler and Armstrong (2020) consider "publics" as an important aspect of the microenvironment. Publics includes any group that has an actual or potential interest in a company's ability to be successful. Financial publics such as banks or investors are important stakeholders, particularly for start-ups. Media publics (e. g. newspapers, tv channels, blogs, and social media influencers) can help or hinder a company's visibility and image.

A proper analysis of the microenvironment is key to understand an industry and anticipate possible developments in the future. Depending on the industry, individual factors are sometimes given more and sometimes less weight.

4.2.2 The Macroenvironment

Broader societal forces that affect the actors in the microenvironment are part of a macroenvironment analysis. These forces can hardly be controlled by one or several companies, but they are fundamental for the development of entire markets and thus to companies' ability to achieve their objectives.

A good framework that covers the most important aspects of a macroenvironment is the PESTEL (or PESTLE) analysis. There are many similar concepts, sometimes referred to as PEST analysis, STEP, or STEEP analysis. PESTEL (or PESTLE) is an acronym. The letters stand for

- P = Political factors: Government policy (e.g. regarding trades or taxation) may impact an industry or a specific organisation.
- E = Economic factors: Wealth, unemployment rates, the overall economic growth and many more factors may directly impact markets and organisations.
- S = Socio-cultural factors: This stands for demographic trends, lifestyle developments and other factors related to needs, motives, and actual behaviour. Those factors are key to understanding potential customers and emerging trends. Adapting to them may give a company a competitive advantage.
- T = Technological factors: Technological innovations can have disruptive power to entire markets and all of its competitors. Keeping an eye on (future) innovations is a must for companies.
- E = Environmental factors: The natural environment has become more important in recent years. This can easily be observed in the many CSR activities of companies. Developing environmentally sustainable strategies requires extensive know-how about environmental factors.
- L = Legal factors: Different territories have different legal requirements. Organisations must understand them and should be prepared for legal changes.

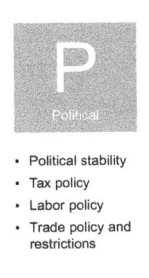

- Political stability
- Tax policy
- Labor policy
- Trade policy and restrictions

Significant cross over with legal factors:

- Economic growth
- Exchange rate
- Inflation rate
- Interest rate
- Unemployment rate
- Consumer purchasing power

- Demographic trends
- (Changes in) lifestyle
- (Changes in) attitudes and values
- Education levels and resources
- Cultural barriers
- Health consciousness
- Career attitudes

- Digital or mobile technology
- Innovations in distribution, manufacturing or logistics
- Activities in R&D (Research and Development)

- Surrounding environment (climate, weather, resources etc.)
- Impact on ecological aspects (e. g. carbon footprint, waste disposal)
- Recycling procedures
- Pressures from NGOs

- Employment laws
- Consumer protection laws
- Copyright and patent laws
- Health and safety laws
- Discrimination laws

Fig. 4.10 PESTEL framework to analyse the macroenvironment. The list of details is not exhaustive and should be supplemented in the specific individual case (cf. Aguilar, 1967)

All of these factors are completely external from a company's perspective. The quality of such an analysis depends strongly on research efforts and on thorough consideration of what information is valid and relevant to an industry.

Figure 4.10 lists in more detail what is meant by each aspect in the PESTEL framework. For illustration purposes, we transfer some macroenvironmental forces to the e-bike industry in Germany and outline exemplary implications for a firm like Cowboy.

Political Forces The democratic structures in Germany are stable. Tax policy is extremely complex and requires companies to pay above-average tax rates compared to some other European countries. Germany is part of the Single European Market. This market is characterised by the four freedoms—free trade in goods, free movement of persons, free movement of capital and free movement of services. For Cowboy, these are favourable conditions to establish and expand their business model in Europe. Britain's exit from the EU, on the other hand, is a negative development for companies like Cowboy.

Economical Forces The pandemic is having a negative economic impact in Germany. The gross domestic product has shrunk. People's uncertainty about financial investments has increased. Compared to many other regions, however, purchasing power in Germany is still high. Several governmental programmes have saved many people from unemployment or large pay cuts. The economy recovered relatively quickly after the initial shock and forecasts for the future are mostly optimistic.

Social-Cultural Forces The pandemic has also led to various changes in attitudes, motives, and buying behaviour of many people. Here are some examples:

- Many people have not spent money on vacations and instead invested in items such as bikes or household items.
- The need for individual mobility without risk of infection has increased. As a result, the bicycle has become significantly more popular.
- Rising real estate prices have driven many young families to the outskirts of cities. For this target group, modern e-bikes are a good choice because they meet the functional criteria and fit the lifestyle.
- There have been significant changes in attitudes and lifestyles, primarily among young professionals with a high education level. In marketing, this consumer type is called LOHAS, which stands for Lifestyles of Health and Sustainability. This segment is growing and represents a major target group for Cowboy.
- Shopping behaviour has also changed significantly. Online shopping has become even more popular, benefiting companies with direct digital sales. Cowboy sells almost exclusively through its own web store.

Technological Forces Cowboy's concept includes to provide "connected bikes" with innovative technical features such as integrated apps, anti-theft-system, GPS locating and integrated detectors for accident notifications. Cowboy's e-bike generates its best value-adding features when combined with a smartphone. The company must therefore always keep an eye on smartphone trends. New production capabilities for electric batteries and other parts of their bike are also highly relevant to the company. If Cowboy misses important technology trends or reacts too slowly, its brand reputation would likely suffer. This is especially true for companies that have modernity and progress anchored in their brand core.

Environmental Factors These are of particular importance to Cowboy, as its target group has a strong environmental awareness. E-bikes are environmentally friendly, as significantly less CO_2 is emitted, and less energy is used through their use. The use of e-bikes also has a significantly lower impact on air quality. For these reasons, European countries are increasingly promoting electromobility. In Germany, for example companies can nowadays use e-bikes (and e-cars) as company vehicles and receive tax benefits. The purchase incentives for consumers and companies increase considerably. Furthermore, bike paths and good surfaces are an important prerequisite for e-bike enjoyment. Fortunately for Cowboy and all other bike manufacturers, the German government intends to significantly improve the network of bike paths and their quality by 2030. Many cities have already launched initiatives to create better conditions for cyclists.

Legal Factors Legal factors are sometimes not listed as a separate category because they have much overlap with the other factors in the PESTEL framework. However, there are specific legal requirements for e-bikes that companies like Cowboy must meet. Due to an EU directive, e-bikes can be used legally in all European countries. However, manufacturers must keep an eye on legal details in all relevant countries and adapt their e-bikes to local regulations if necessary. For example in Germany the motors in e-bikes are only allowed to have a limited power and only support up to 25 km/h. For such e-bikes, there is no license plate or driver's license requirement. There is currently no age restriction. If Cowboy increases the motor power, their e-bike would fall under a different category with age restrictions, driver's license requirements, and more. Cowboy's holder for smartphones and their app design must also meet specifications in order to be approved for use in road traffic.

These are just a few examples of factors to consider in an environmental analysis. The described factors and forces are not independent. They cannot always be clearly delineated. Some factors reinforce each other, such as environmental policy and tax incentives for e-bikes. Other factors point in opposite directions and must be weighed against each other.

A good environmental analysis should enable you to derive threats and opportunities. It is an excellent pre-stage for a SWOT analysis, which matches a company's internal strengths and weaknesses with external threats and opportunities in the environment.

References

Aguilar, F. J. (1967). *Scanning the business environment.* MacMillan Co..

Booker, B. (2017). *7 epic fails that consumer testing can help you avoid.* Accessed July 20, 2021, from https://www.askattest.com/blog/articles/7-epic-fails-that-consumer-testing-can-help-you-avoid

Brunello, J. (2018). *Personas: How to create personas with secondary data.* DAAD.

Christensen, C. M., & Raynor, M. E. (2003). *The innovator's solution* (1st ed.). Harvard Business Review Press.

Clark, S. (2020). *What Can Social Listening Do to Improve CX?* Accessed July 25, 2021, from https://www.cmswire.com/customer-experience/what-can-social-listening-do-to-improve-cx/

Dalton, J. (2017). *Ethnographic study: The how at the heart of customer intimacy.* https://thrivethinking.com/2017/01/24/ethnographic-study-the-how-of-customer-intimacy/

Estey, T. (2019). *The art & science of ethnographic marketing research.* https://medium.com/@tasha.estey/the-art-science-of-ethnographic-marketing-research-49e703234c00

De Keyser, A., Verleye, K., Lemon, K. N., Keiningham, T., & Klaus, P. (2015). A Framework for Understanding and Managing the CX. Marketing Science Institute Working Paper Series 2015, Report No. 15–121, Marketing Science Institute: Cambridge, MA.

Gibbons, S. (2019). *Empathy mapping: The first step in design thinking.* Accessed July 15, 2021, from https://www.nngroup.com/articles/empathy-mapping/

Goffin, K., Varnes, C., Van der Hoven, C., & Koners, U. (2012). Beyond the voice of the customer: Ethnographic market research. *Research Technology Management, 55*(4), 45–53. Accessed August 4, 2021, from https://www.jstor.org/stable/26586628

Gray, D. (2017). *Updated empathy map canvas.* Accessed July 12, 2021, from https://medium.com/the-xplane-collection/updated-empathy-map-canvas-46df22df3c8a

Häusel, H. (2011). *The Scientific Foundation of the Limbic Approach*. Gruppe Nymphenburg.

Häusel, H. (2019). *Neuromarketing: Erkenntnisse der Hirnforschung für Markenführung, Werbung und Verkauf.*

Interaction Design Foundation. (2016). Accessed July 22, 2021, from https://www.interaction-design.org/literature/article/laddering-questions-drilling-down-deep-and-moving-sideways-in-ux-research

Kahl, A. (2020). *Problem validation: Making sure you're talking to the right people*. Accessed July 20, 2021, from https://thebootstrappedfounder.com/problem-validation/

Kahneman, D., & Lovallo, D. (1993). Timid choices and bold forecasts: A cognitive perspective on risk taking. *Management Science, 39*(1), 17–31. http://www.jstor.org/stable/2661517

Kotler, P., & Armstrong, G. (2014). *Principles of marketing*. Global Edition (17th ed). Pearson.

Kotler, P., & Armstrong, G. (2020). *Principles of marketing*. Global Edition (18th ed.). Pearson.

Lemon, K. N., & Verhoef, P. (2016). Understanding customer experience throughout the customer journey. *Journal of Marketing, 80*, 69–96.

McKinsey and Company. (2017). *Customer Experience: New capabilities, new audiences, new opportunities*. Accessed July 5, 2021, from https://www.mckinsey.de/~/media/mckinsey/industries/public%20and%20social%20sector/our%20insights/cx%20compendium%202017/customer-experience-compendium-july-2017.pdf

Newman, D., & McClimans, F. (2019). *Experience 2030: The future of customer experience EMEA*. https://www.sas.com/content/dam/SAS/documents/marketing-whitepapers-ebooks/third-party-whitepapers/en/futurum-experience-2030-emea-110977.pdf

Porta, M. (2021). *How to define your target market*. https://www.inc.com/guides/2010/06/defining-your-target-market.html

Porter, M. E. (1979). How competitive forces shape strategy. *Harvard Business Review, 57*(2), 137–145.

Porter, M. E. (2008). The five competitive forces that shape strategy. *Harvard Business Review, 88*(1), 79–93.

Rehfeld, M. (2019). *Creating an emotional tie with the Limbic° Map*. Accessed July 12, 2021, from https://www.mashup-communications.de/en/2019/04/creating-an-emotional-tie-with-the-limbic-map/

Risdon, C. (2012). *Anatomy of an experience map*. Accessed July 15, 2021, from https://articles.uie.com/experience_map/

Sarstedt, M., & Mooi, E. (2019). Introduction to market research. Springer Texts in Business and Economics. In *A concise guide to market research* (3rd edn., chapter 1, pages 1–9). Springer.

Schebrova, A. (2018). *Multiple personas on one customer journey map*. Accessed June 17, 2021, from https://uxpressia.com/blog/multiple-personas-on-one-customer-journey-map

Statista. (2020). *Number of social network users worldwide from 2017 to 2025 (in billions)*. Accessed August 4, 2021, from https://www.statista.com/statistics/278414/number-of-worldwide-social-network-users/

Stegemann, M. (2021). *Customer Journey (Part 2)*. Accessed July 15, 2021, from https://www.youtube.com/watch?v=ogSK0faw064

Stickdorn, M., Hormess, M. E., Lawrence, A., & Schneider, J. (2018). *This is service design methods* (1st ed.). O'Reilly Media.

Ulwick, A. W. (2016). *Jobs to be done*. Idea Bite Press.

Venkatesh, A., Crockett, D., Cross, S., & Chen, S. (2017). Ethnography for marketing and consumer research. *Foundations and Trends® in Marketing, 10*, 61–151. https://doi.org/10.1561/1700000043

Wilcox, J. (2017). *How to interview your customers*. Accessed July 26, 2021, from https://customerdevlabs.com/2013/11/05/how-i-interview-customers/

5

Outside-In: Defining the CX-Centric Business DNA—The Why, How, and What of a Start-Up

Customer experience does not improve until it becomes a key priority and a part of the company's core to reflect that (Meyer & Schwager, 2007), and the best way to execute that is to integrate CX into the company DNA. The first building block of the corporate DNA is the customer experience, which the customer should experience in the context of his interaction with the corporate services. As a core element, these should have an impact on all other corporate concepts and services. The company DNA is like the ink in a glass of water that spreads to all corners of the company (see Fig. 5.1).

Simon Sinek (2009) uses "The Golden Circle" to explain how companies successfully differentiate themselves through the creation and communication of their value proposition. According to the model, companies must first understand the reason for their existence, i.e. the belief, purpose or the "Why?". With the "Why" in place, companies can then proceed to define how they can differentiate themselves, which primary includes its strategy. At this point, a well-defined "why" and "how" should seamlessly lead to the answer "what", which focuses on the concrete products and services the companies should offer in the market to achieve the "why". According to Sinek, it is important to employ the inside-out perspective as "people don't buy what you do, they buy why you do it".

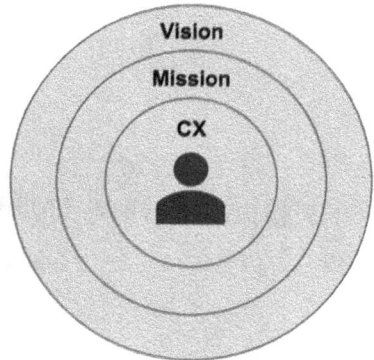

Fig. 5.1 CX at the core of company DNA

5.1 Why?

The question "Why?" can be answered by understanding the specific experiences that a customer should have in his or her interactions with the company. For example a customer at Apple should be able to feel trendy and innovative, a customer at Airbnb, local and cosmopolitan, a customer at Disney happy and in the flow. Therefore, it is important for companies to ask: "What kind of customer experiences do we want to create for our customers"? The answer lies in the insights gathered from Chap. 4. With a well-defined core, it is then crucial to root this in the company culture, and spread it throughout the various departments and processes.

5.1.1 Mission

The mission is the first corporate concept in which the customer experience manifests itself. This is particularly important because the mission represents the meaning and purpose of the company, and what it seeks to accomplish in the larger environment. The mission statement sets the direction and boundaries for day to day operations of an organisation and its strategic planning. It supports the organisation in moving the teams towards the company's goals (Darbi, 2012), and serves as an

5 Outside-In: Defining the CX-Centric Business DNA—The Why...

"invisible hand" that guides people in the organisation. In addition, the mission statement is usually more oriented to the present and focuses on the "how" to achieve the goal. Increasingly, mission statements are more connected to the business purpose and market needs instead of the business offering, and sees an increasing reference to larger purposes such as sustainability and social values (Stegemann, 2021).

IKEA's mission statement is highly specific and describes the "how" to achieve their vision: "Our business idea supports [our] vision by offering a wide range of well-designed, functional home furnishing products at prices so low that as many people as possible will be able to afford them". (IKEA, 2021).

5.1.2 Vision

On the other hand, the vision represents an ambitious and more inwardly focused goal that the company would like to achieve in the long term (Kreutzer, 2019, p.33). It is more oriented towards the future and formulated as an end state: where does the company want to be? A vision statement is often more inspiring and encompasses the value of the company, and may include the contribution of the company to society. A well-defined vision ensures a positive identification of employees with the company and motivates them with regard to the goal to be achieved.

IKEA's vision statement effectively showcases the end goal and the "why" behind their business: "To create a better everyday life for the many people" (IKEA, 2021).

5.2 How?

With a well-defined "why", the next key step which follows is the translation of the mission and vision into a business model geared towards specific market objectives. In order to build up the business and brand in a customer experience-centric manner, a suitable business and brand model should be defined to support the creation of strong customer experiences.

5.2.1 Business Model

While it is important to focus on understanding customer needs and wants, companies must not overlook the importance of its business model and capabilities (Keiningham et al., 2020). A company's business model should support and enable it to achieve its vision and mission ("why"). Companies need to define their business model, which is "a framework for finding a systematic way to unlock long-term value for an organisation while delivering value to customers and capturing value through monetisation strategies" (Cuofano, 2020a).

Business Model Canvas

Start-ups move at rapid pace and thus require a simplified yet comprehensive way to map out their business model to facilitate strategic planning and pitching. Many lean start-ups have adopted the well-known Business Model Canvas (Osterwalder & Pigneur, 2010), which is a structured and visual framework for the identification and summary of the relevant components: Customer Segments, Value Propositions, Channels, Customer Relationships, Revenue Streams, Key Activities, Key Resources, Key Partnerships and Cost Structure of a customer strategy on a single page (see Fig. 5.2). This canvas is highly recommended for start-ups that have validated their ideas and are further down the development stages as it offers a deep framework that looks into concrete areas such as key partners, activities, and resources, which are essential building blocks of a business.

The Business Model Canvas is divided into three blocks: desirability, viability, and feasibility. Desirability consists of customer segments, value propositions, channels, and customer relationships. This block places an emphasis on whether there is a fit between a company's offerings and the market (Strategyzer, 2019). Firstly, companies should begin with defining the customer segments which they would like to target. This chapter can be filled with the information gathered from Sect. 4.1.1. Next, with the target group in mind, companies need to define their value proposition, which is the value they are creating for their target group, for instance, pain relievers and gain creators for the target group's job. With

5 Outside-In: Defining the CX-Centric Business DNA—The Why...

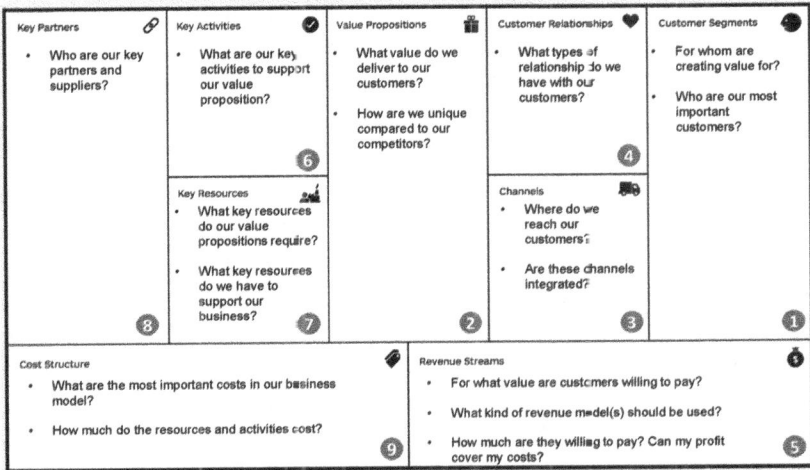

Fig. 5.2 Business model canvas (adapted from Strategyzer, 2020)

a clear picture of the target group and the company's value proposition, companies should define the channels to reach customers and the relationship between the companies and their target group. The channels can include both online and offline and are usually a combination of different platforms such as social media and website. On the other hand, customer relationships focus more strongly on the type of relationships the companies share with customers, for instance, the type of atmosphere, customer service and interactions that companies should have with their customers (Jeffries, 2018).

With a business that provides product-market fit, it is then crucial to identify if the business model is viable, or in other words, profitable. Viability consists of cost structure and revenue streams and essentially represents the bottom line of the business. Firstly, it is important to identify potential revenue streams and revenue models which the company can leverage on (Jeffries, 2018). A revenue stream is a company's single source of income, e.g. sale of product, services, and advertisement spaces, while a revenue model is the strategy to manage the revenue streams (Founder Institute, 2018). Some of the most common revenue models include transaction-based, subscription, commission, freemium, affiliate, and advertising revenue. These models will be elaborated in the following sections:

Transaction-Based Revenue is the most direct revenue model where companies charge a certain price for providing a service or product each time. This revenue model is extremely simple and straightforward. For instance, Apple charges a specific price for the Macbooks, iMacs, and iPhones it sells (Founder Institute, 2018).

Companies can also employ the *commission revenue* model, where they earn a commission fee instead of the full profit with each transaction. This revenue model is commonly used in online marketplaces where the companies earning the commission act as an intermediary between the buyer and seller. In this context, the commission earned by the company can be seen as a reward for helping the seller receive a successful transaction. A commission revenue model can be implemented without having to offer products or services, but this also means that the revenue generated is limited and difficult to scale (Nesvit, 2021). For example Apple charges a percentage commission for every paid app and in-app feature purchased by users.

With a *subscription-based revenue* model, instead of paying one time for the use of the products and services, customers pay for over a longer period of time, usually on a monthly or annual basis. A subscription-based model allows for companies to maintain a more regular and certain cash flow. However, for a company to be able to implement such a revenue model, its product or service needs to command a regular use demand and be sufficiently useful that users will want to use and pay for it on a regular basis. For instance, Apple services, including Apple TV, Apple Music, Apple Arcade, iCloud, Apple News+ and Apple Fitness, are all offered on a subscription where customers pay a certain monthly or yearly fee. In addition, it is also common for companies to offer a more attractive deal for higher commitment subscription, i.e. annual subscription is more affordable than a year of monthly subscription (Founder Institute, 2018).

The *freemium model* is being increasingly used by companies offering digital services. It works by offering the basic features or services for free and charging for advanced features. Such a model is rising in popularity due to the ability to allow customers to try the product without a financial commitment and attracting them to pay for an important add-on later. However, this model requires effective strategisation to determine what to offer such that it is enough for customers to see the value in the product but not too much that customers are comfortably satisfied without paying for the premium features. Also, companies need to consistently think of ways to convert free users into paying customers (Founder Institute, 2018). For instance, iCloud provides 5 GB of storage space for free. Once users begin to rely on the storage space for various purposes, they will be enticed to pay extra to increase their capacity and to reduce the switching costs.

The *affiliate revenue model* is another popular revenue model for digital businesses where companies earn a commission by promoting links to other products and services on their site. The model usually works with a tracking system for the company selling the products and services to track if the successful purchase comes from an affiliate site. Commission is then paid out to the company depending on the transactions which originated from the company site. This can also be used in combination with advertisements (Founder Institute, 2018). The use of this revenue model does not require companies to own any services or products as they simply need to link to the actual businesses. However, this also means that the revenue generated through this model is often more limited as the commission fees are usually not too huge. Often, affiliate sites attract traffic with their content which means time and effort need to be invested in this respect. For instance, The Wirecutter, a product review website, produces high-quality content on electronics, gadgets, and consumer goods which helps consumers make better purchase decisions. The site produces content such as "The Best Portable Bluetooth Speaker" and links the relevant sites offering affiliate fees. The Wirecutter then earns revenue when a user purchases by clicking on the affiliate link (Breton, 2020).

Advertisement-based revenue is usually a supplementary revenue model which involves the selling of advertisement spaces on digital platforms such as website or e-commerce site to feature an external company or brand for increased exposure. This revenue model is easy to implement and can lead to significant revenue if the company's digital space is high in traffic. However, it is important to note that this revenue model can only be effective when the platform has high traffic, and attention should be given to the type of advertisements and brands which the company allows to feature. Advertisements that come across as annoying or incompatible with the platform can pose detriment to the overall customer experience, which can reduce clickthrough rates and lower conversion (Founder Institute, 2018). For instance, Apple sells ad spaces on the App Store to app providers who would like to be featured on the main page.

When analysing the various revenue model options, it is important to consider several factors such as scalability, recurrence, profitability per transaction and ease of implementation (see Fig. 5.3). For instance, recurring revenue models such as the subscription model allows for a more predictable and consistent revenue flow, which allows for more stable growth investment. Businesses with such a model also usually entails a more scalable business model as the product or service is relatively standardised, allowing for a disproportionally increase in revenue against costs. However, on the other hand, companies also need to consider the complexity involved with recurring revenue as they usually require a more complicated setup and more mature development stage. On the other hand, while a transactional-based revenue offers less predictability, it usually allows for higher profitability per transaction, which means less quantity sold is required as compared to the subscription or commission

Revenue Model	Description	Examples	Scalability	Recurrence & Predictability	Profitability Per Transaction	Ease of Implementation
Transactional	A certain price including margin is charged for providing a service or product each time	Macbooks, iPhones	◐	◐	●	◐
Commission	A commission fee instead of the full profit is earned with each transaction	Apple App Store	◐	◐	◕	●
Subscription	Use of product or service is charged for over a longer period of time (e.g. monthly)	Apple TV	●	●	◕	◐
Freemium	Basic features are offered for free and advanced features are charged.	Apple iCloud	●	●	◐	◕
Affiliate	Companies earn a commission by promoting links to other products and services on their site.	The Wirecutter	●	◕	◕	●
Advertisement	A certain price is charged for the sale of advertisement spaces on digital platforms.	Apple App Store Ads	●	◐	◐	●

Fig. 5.3 Comparison of revenue models

model. At the initial stages, companies may wish to focus on a single revenue model in consideration of the development stages. As companies become more developed over time and expand to provide more value offers, it is common to adopt multiple revenue streams and models, as illustrated with the case of Apple.

After the selection of the appropriate and relevant revenue model(s), companies also need to identify the different cost areas such as personnel, marketing, and technological after looking at the key resources, partners, and activities in the next chapter. By looking at both revenue and costs, companies are able to create forecasts such as required investments, cost per acquisition, customer lifetime value and breakeven points. In addition, companies also employ these figures to calculate price sensitivity and create effective pricing strategies (Cuofano, 2020b).

A desirable and viable business idea must lastly be feasible to achieve. Feasibility consists of key partners, key activities and resources. This block mainly identifies the required resources and helps companies perform the check on whether they have access to the right resources and partners to carry out their activities. Key resources consist of manpower, equipment, and assets, which are fundamental to the functioning of the business. Key partners, on the other hand, refer to companies and people who support the business, e.g. suppliers, transport partners and marketing agencies. Last but not least, key activities related to the core processes which must be carried out to deliver value to customers (Strategyzer, 2019).

It is important to note that the nine sections are highly interdependent, and companies should aim to ensure that their analyses integrate the different sections together. By doing so, companies can become more focused and lean as the canvas can highlight potentially overlooked activities and resources which are fundamental to success and help companies revaluate and reduce expenses that do not deliver value. The outcome of the canvas should be an effective and thorough business model.

Lean Canvas

For companies just starting up, it is recommended to use the Lean Canvas (see Fig. 5.4), which includes the problem-solution definition as achieving product-market fit is core to every young start-up as it puts more focus on finding a strong fit between the business and the customer

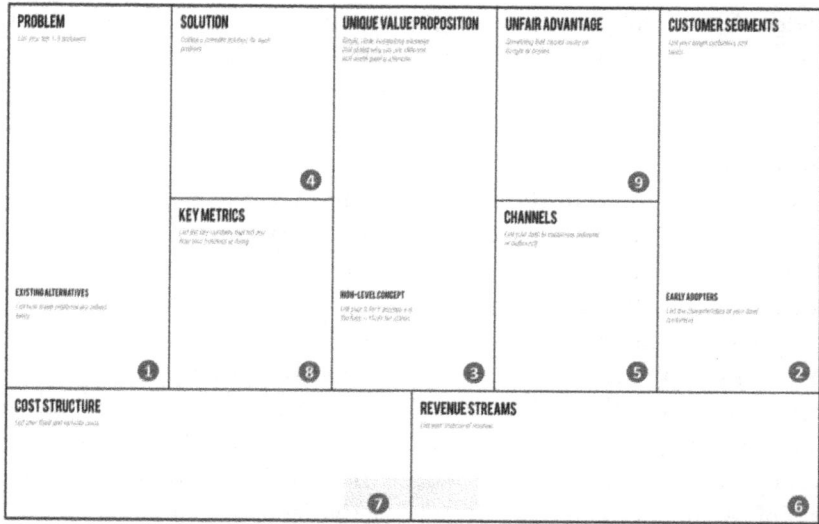

Fig. 5.4 The lean canvas (adapted from Maurya, 2010)

problem, which is fundamental to creating strong customer experiences. Ash Maurya's belief that "life is too short to build something nobody wants" summarises the essence of the Lean Canvas—focus on product-market fit.

The Lean Canvas replaces the key partners, key activities and key resources with problem, solution, and key metrics. Instead of focusing on feasibility, the Lean Canvas is aimed at helping companies identify their riskiest assumptions in the business model—business validation. Without market validation and traction from potential customers, companies can end up vesting resources on developing products with no real market demand and eventually also struggle with securing investments and resources. As such, the Lean Canvas draws the focus of companies to achieving idea validation before committing huge amounts of resources for further development (Skowrow, 2020).

As such, companies need to first identify problems, followed by customer segments that resonate strongly with the problems. After which, companies should define their unique value proposition and ideate on solutions that can help to deliver the intended value. Before this, the canvas also encourages companies to study their competition and existing solutions to build a business with a unique and improved differentiation. As a start, it is important to note that the solution does not have to be thorough but a rough guide. With the basic solution in mind, several rounds of iterative user testing can be carried out to gather insights, refine the solution and test again.

The other key differences from the business model canvas are the unfair advantage and key metrics. According to the lean canvas, it is important for companies to identify competitive advantages which they have over potential competitors, as these can influence the long-term sustainability of companies. If a company has an unfair advantage such as strategic partnerships, patents, and more, the company is less likely to be imitated and can hold a stronger position in the market for a longer time horizon. With all areas well defined, it is important for companies to finally identify a few metrics which need to be tracked to ensure business success, for instance, number of downloads and sales. Without key metrics, companies may find it challenging to gauge their performances and are thus clueless about the areas which require improvements (Skowrow, 2020).

The canvas also presents the business model in a concise manner which facilitates user testing and pitching, which is key to validating the business idea before proceeding to identify concrete partners and resources. A business idea with concrete building blocks but without proper validation is equally far from the finishing line. The outcome of the lean canvas is a validated business model with product-market fit.

Business Flywheel
As companies define their business model and strategy, it is important to take the flywheel into consideration. The flywheel explains the success strategy of a company and how the business can become easier and less costly to run in the long term.

The example of Amazon's flywheel as illustrated in Fig. 5.5 will be used to explain the Flywheel concept. In the case of Amazon, by increasing the sellers on marketplace platform, the platform selection offered to customers will increase, which leads to improvements of customer experience. With improved customer experience, platform traffic will increase and in turn attract more sellers to Amazon. This flywheel model shows the four

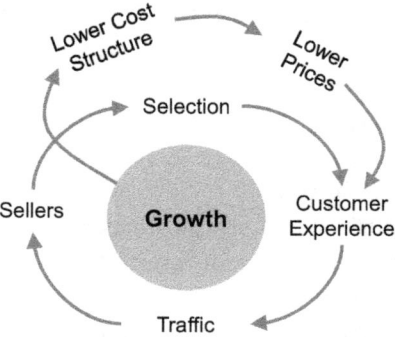

Fig. 5.5 The Amazon flywheel (adapted from Bezos, 2001)

main forces of Amazon driving its growth. As long as one of the four forces is strengthened, improvements in the other three will also follow. In the long run, overall growth improves Amazon's cost structure due to economies of scale which will then lead to lower prices and an improved customer experience which again keeps the virtuous cycle going (Cuofano, 2021).

Every company should look into designing its own flywheel that is unique to itself and tailored to its business model. By having a flywheel business model, companies will have an easier time scaling up and experience an exponential revenue growth. In order to define a flywheel that is unique to the business, this three-step process in Fig. 5.6 can be employed.

Firstly, companies need to ensure that there is alignment between the product, market, and channel, which essentially means a feasible business model. Following that, companies need to identify areas in which they can build their competitive advantages on by analysing the three aspects of their business: configuration (company DNA), offering (customer solutions) and experience (customer experience) (see Fig. 5.6).

During the analysis, companies should identify their strengths and weaknesses influencing their growth and investigate potential improvements which can support in further enhancing their strengths or overcoming their weaknesses. The best 4–6 of the identified improvement areas will serve as key drivers for the Flywheel. Lastly, companies need to map out their flywheel with the elements identified and test the concept

5 Outside-In: Defining the CX-Centric Business DNA—The Why...

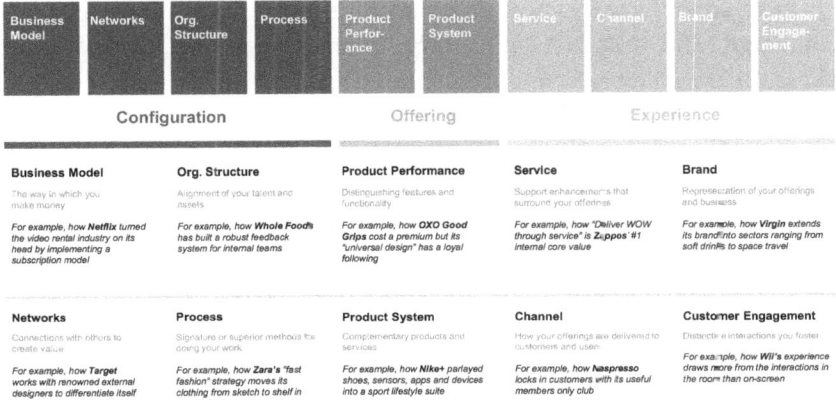

Fig. 5.6 Elements of the flywheel: ten types of innovation (adapted from Keeley et al. 2013; Kylliäinen, 2019)

by focusing on the growth levers and measuring if increased efforts on those levers lead to a self-sustaining flywheel. It is important to note that companies can use more than one attempt before arriving at their functioning flywheel model. However, once the flywheel model defined is proven to work, the company will be able to focus its business strategy and achieve long-term scalability and growth.

With a more thorough definition of the solution and offering, companies should revisit the one-sentence pitch defined in Sect. 3.2.1 and make the necessary refinements to better reflect the company offers. At this point, it is important to carry out the first tests to validate the solution ideas. The big question here is "does anyone even want the product?" Most companies at this stage are not ready and not recommended to create a real product before the idea is validated. On the other hand, companies may find it challenging to validate an idea without a product. To overcome this problem, a Concierge minimum viable product (Concierge MVP) can be employed by substituting the real product with a human (O'Malley, 2020). The objective of the Concierge MVP is to allow companies to test their product ideas without compromising on the details and without having to invest in product development. For example if the test product is a fitness service marketplace app that recommends users the most suitable fitness service based on the user's characteristics, the Concierge MVP will involve having a human to do the manual job of asking for the characteristics of the user, consolidating the characteristics of the user and manually identifying the most suitable fitness service. Through the process of delivering the MVP, companies will uncover various insights about their customers, problems with the processes and most importantly, whether customers see value in the solution offered. With the new insights gathered regarding the solution idea, companies can then revisit the initial solution and refine it to better meet the needs of the target group.

5.2.2 Brand Identity

The brand identity expresses what a specific brand stands for and serves an important role as it forms the basis of a brand strategy (Esch, 2017), e.g. communication strategy, product development, design visuals, and helps to ensure a consistent brand image across different channels. To define a brand's identity, it is necessary to understand the fundamental criteria which it is comprised of. Firstly, the self-image, which is an internal perception of the brand by its managers and employees. Secondly, identity-reflecting attributes such as corporate design and store environment which the brand uses to convey its identity to others (Schmitt & Rogers, 2008).

For defining the brand identity, a brand model should be used. There are several different models which exist in literature, but this chapter will focus on the two popular brand models—Esch's brand steering wheel (2017) and Kapferer's Brand Identity Prism (2012) as they comprehensively cover the key perspectives of brand identity.

The brand steering wheel developed by Esch (see Fig. 5.7) provides a framework to align the hard and soft facts of a brand. Hard facts, which can also be understood as what a company offers, are represented by the left of the wheel, which includes the brand benefits and attributes. On the other hand, the right side of the wheel represents the soft facts of the brand, which relates to how the company is and are associated with emotions and impressions (ESCH, n.d.). The steering wheel allows

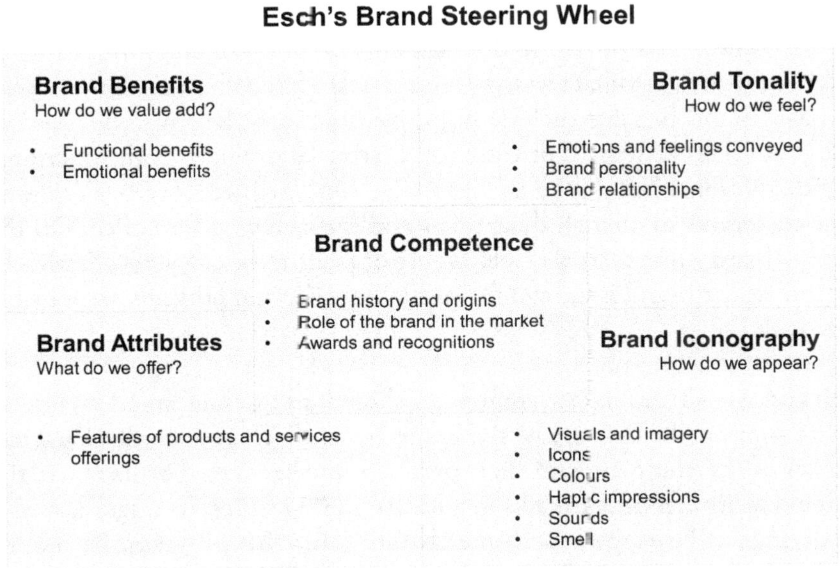

Esch's Brand Steering Wheel

Brand Benefits
How do we value add?

- Functional benefits
- Emotional benefits

Brand Tonality
How do we feel?

- Emotions and feelings conveyed
- Brand personality
- Brand relationships

Brand Competence

- Brand history and origins
- Role of the brand in the market
- Awards and recognitions

Brand Attributes
What do we offer?

- Features of products and services offerings

Brand Iconography
How do we appear?

- Visuals and imagery
- Icons
- Colours
- Haptic impressions
- Sounds
- Smell

Fig. 5.7 The brand steering wheel (adapted from Esch, 2017)

companies to align the general aspects of the brand, including its products and services, to deliver the intended brand to customers.

Brand Competence Brand competence is defined as "consumers' considerations that a brand has the ability and skills to meet consumers' intentions, and it emphasizes on a brand's competitiveness, intelligence, and skills." (Xue et al., 2020). Companies can define their brand competence by identifying their core brand characteristics which can include their brand's history, origins, market role and central assets. For instance, Starbucks boasts of a rich heritage and was established first in Seattle in 1971. It has become the world's biggest coffeehouse chain, with over 32,000 stores worldwide (Starbucks, 2021). The company has also received several awards such as "Best Company for Women", "Best Company Work-Life Balance", and more (Comparably, 2021). Identifying brand competence is crucial as it is strongly associated with perceived trust and reliability.

Brand Benefits
Companies need to define the benefits which the brand would like to deliver to its customers as they are the real reason for a customer's purchase. Brand benefits include objective-functional benefits and psychological social benefits. For instance, Starbucks provides both functional and emotional benefits to its customers. On one hand, Starbucks allows its customers to quench their thirst and their craving for coffee. On the other hand, customers also feel a sense of pride to be carrying a Starbucks drink as the brand is known for its high quality and ethically responsible process.

Brand Attributes Next, companies should also define brand attributes that support the delivery of the brand benefits. These include characteristics of the company and their products and services. For instance, the brand attributes of Starbucks include its 32,000 stores, its huge customer offerings of beverages, food, merchandise, rewards program, its mobile application and more. Brand attributes are important as they are often where customer interactions with the brand take place.

Brand Tonality Brand tonality includes emotions and feelings associated with a brand which can be explored through its personality traits, experiences, and relations provided by the brand to its customers. Companies need to define this, as emotions and feelings generated by a brand can strongly influence a customer perception of the brand. While defining the tonality, it is important for companies to take into consideration the type of relationship it would like to build with its customers. For instance, since Starbucks' mission is to "inspire and nurture the human spirit" (Starbucks, 2015), it delivers that through the creation of culture of warmth and belonging, which makes the brand come across as open-minded, chill and loves to enjoy the pleasures of life. Companies can also use the Limbic Map in Sect. 4.1.2 as an inspiration for positioning their brands and creating their brand tonality to fit their target customers. Companies should ask themselves which emotional purchase motives are currently present in their target group and which motives it would like to address. For example the Becks brand could be placed in the middle-up area of the Limbic Map because the brand appeals to motives such as adventure, spontaneity, or variety.

Brand Iconography The brand iconography supports the delivery of the brand through visuals and communications, such as logo, brand colours, taglines, and more. When defining the iconography, companies need to ensure that it aligns with the other components of the wheel. For instance, Starbucks has an iconic Siren logo with the green mermaid, which is derived from the association with Seattle, a port city, and the transportation of coffee. Its brand colours of white and deep green have also been inspired by the concepts of healing, nature, and protection, which is well-aligned with their ethical corporate behaviour.

The other model, Kapferer's Brand Identity Prism (Kapferer, 2009), also provides a comprehensive framework to enable companies to create a distinctive brand identity. Unlike the Brand Steering Wheel, the Brand Identity Prism focuses less on the offerings of the brand but rather on the way the brand presents itself, particularly in the field of communication. As such, this model is useful for companies looking to create a precise imagery and a personal way of communicating with its target customers (Nugno, 2019). This model consists of six building blocks: physique, personality, culture, relationship, reflection, and self-image, which are grouped according to two dimensions: picture of sender-picture of receiver and externalisation-internalisation (see Fig. 5.8).

According to the model, it is important for companies to ensure a match between the perception of the sender (brand) and the receiver (customer), and that a brand does not simply express itself externally but also incorporates the elements in the internal management of the brand. Companies that are able to strategically align these components will be able to create strong brand identities with their target group.

Brand Physique Firstly, companies need to define the physique of the brand, which refers to physical attributes of the brand. This can be likened to the brand attributes and iconography in the Brand Steering Wheel. Specifically, companies should define the set of physical features which they want to evoke in consumer minds upon hearing the brand name. To define this, companies can ask the following questions: how should the brand look like? What can it be used for? How can it be made easily recognisable?

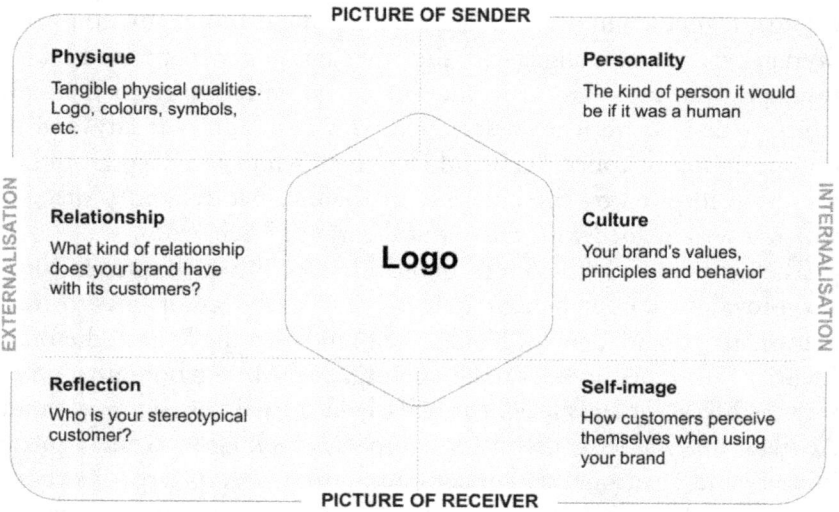

Fig. 5.8 The brand identity prism (adapted from Kapferer, 2012)

Brand Personality Secondly, apart from the appearance of the brand, it is also important for companies to define the brand personality as it determines the way the brand speaks, writes, acts, and more. Companies should liken their brand to humans while defining their character and traits. For instance, Porsche's personality can be defined as ambitious, bold, fierce, and dynamic.

Culture Next, culture often sets the basis for a brand's behaviour, and relates to the values and beliefs with which the brand is associated to. For instance, Mercedes-Benz is strongly associated with its country of origin, Germany, and is strongly tied to the high-quality manufacturing and durability of German engineering. In addition, Toyota has set up a corporate culture that embeds Japanese culture concepts to guide the daily operations of the brand and company.

Relationship Following that, companies should also define the relationship it aims to have with its customers as it determines the communication strategy, e.g. how a brand connects with its audience. As mentioned earlier, Starbucks's mission is to "inspire and nurture the human spirit", which places emphasis on building emotional connection with its customers. As such, it looks to create a supportive and close friendship with its customers.

Reflection The fifth element, reflection, relates to how a brand depicts its target customers, especially in brand communications. For example Coca-Cola often features young, active, and fun teenagers to create a desired association with energy and happiness. It is important to note that the reflection does not have to reflect the brand's real target customers but rather how it wants to be associated.

Self-Image Lastly, companies should also define the self-image element, which is how individuals see themselves in a specific brand. By understanding how consumers perceive themselves when using the brand, companies can use this knowledge to create communications that consumers can relate to and resonate with. For example research has found that Lacoste customers perceive themselves as a member of a sporty community even if they are not actively into sports. With this knowledge, Lacoste created a brand that conveys an active and preppy lifestyle with which its users identify with, even though they may not lead those lifestyles.

While the brand steering wheel helps to create a brand direction and ensures alignment across marketing and communication activities, it provides less guidance on the exact factors which companies should take into consideration when defining their brand identity. On the other hand, the Kapferer's Brand Identity Prism includes additional components such as brand culture, customer reflection and self-image, which are more specific and focused. The Brand Identity Prism, on the other hand, lacks the brand benefits, which were argued to be the main reason for purchase. Both models can also be said to lack the aspect of engagement that a brand should generate, especially in digital times. As seen, the models have their individual advantages and disadvantages. The specific brand model which is best suited for a company must be assessed on a company-specific basis. Adaptations of familiar brand models should therefore be made based on the relevant context so that they meet the requirements of today (Kapferer, 2012). At this point, it is also important for companies to test if the defined brand identity is well-received by its target group and if individual components are well-aligned to deliver the brand identity.

5.2.3 Organisational Goal Setting

To ensure that the start-up is developing in a right and a lean way, it is necessary for companies to set specific business goals such that they are able to focus and work towards something concrete. According to Bruhn (2018), a well-defined goal can serve the following functions:

- *Steering function:* The planning of measures can be based on the defined objectives.
- *Coordination function:* Goals simplify understanding between different business units and people.
- *Control function:* Targets form the basis for evaluating the measures implemented.
- *Motivational function:* Goals provide orientation and meaning. Without goals, there is no success.

To define an effective goal, companies can adopt the SMART goal framework to ensure that goals set are specific, measurable, achievable, relevant, and time bound (Cothran & Wysocki, 2005). Firstly, companies need to define the exact outcome they want to attain, for instance, achieve an NPS value of the target group of 70. Next, companies need to ensure that the goal is measurable such that they can determine success by comparing against the measurement, for instance, to calculate the NPS by conducting customer satisfaction surveys. Thirdly, the goal should be achievable, which means companies should have a clear and feasible idea of how they can attain the goal, for instance, the implementation of a live feedback channel for users to express their concerns to the

5   Outside-In: Defining the CX-Centric Business DNA—The Why...

company in live time such that the company can react in time to improve customer experience. Fourthly, the goal needs to be relevant to the overall company objectives, for instance, an increase in NPS to 70 will increase customer advocacy and loyalty which will lead to long-term profitability. Lastly, the goal should be time-specific, for instance, to be achieved by the end of June 2021.

It is important to define goals on different levels and structure them well. The balance score card uses the four dimensions customer, finance, internal processes and organisation. For start-ups that do not yet earn revenues nor have a well-defined organization, the SOR model provides a great framework to define goals on a psychological as well as response level. Companies can effortlessly set a goal to improve customer satisfaction, but that does not inform them on what needs to be done to achieve the goal. Here, the stimulus organism response (SOR) model (see Fig. 5.9) can be used to identify actionable tasks from the bigger goals. The SOR model is made up of three parts: customer-specific stimuli, psychological constructs (organism) and market goals (response).

This model targets two levels that should be addressed by one or more stimuli (experience elements): a psychological and a behavioural target. To use this model, companies should ask themselves the following three questions:

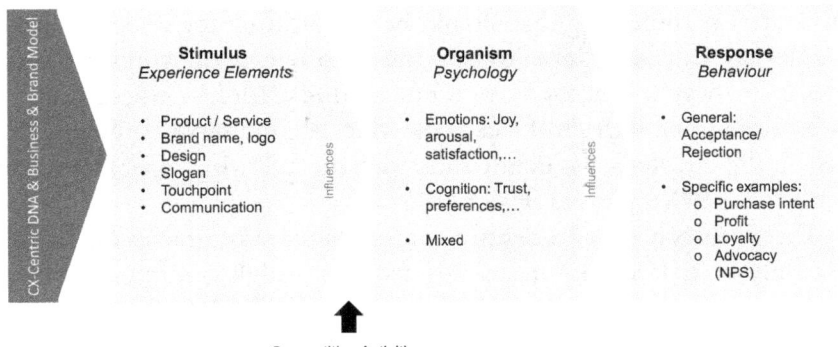

Fig. 5.9 Stimulus organism response model for structuring goals (adapted from Bruhn, 2018, p.36)

- What behaviour do they want to see their customers exhibit? (e.g. To increase app downloads by 20%)
- What customer experiences must be orchestrated for the abovementioned behaviour to happen? What kind of customer emotions and thoughts needs to be evoked? (e.g. Company needs to be perceived as credible and reliable)
- What kind of experience elements do we need to design in order to provide the abovementioned customer experiences, thoughts, or emotions? (e.g. Company should display their reviews and ratings, and implement money-back guarantee)

The questions from point 2 and 3 may need to be answered with the help of customer research. With the answers in place, companies will have a clear visual representation of what they are trying to achieve and measure. From here, the process can also be worked backwards to identify the respective stimulus or experience elements, which need to be implemented to give rise to the intended emotions or response.

5.2.4 Leadership Culture

The culture and principles of collaborative working have been proven to be one of the key success factors for any organisation (Inpowercoaching, 2019). Ideally, this culture does not arise randomly or in an erratic way. Instead, it is something that should be managed by the leaders. Hiring employees who are believed to have the same values and working principles is one way to "manage" corporate culture. 21done—the start-up of two of the three authors of this book which should serve as the practice case in this chapter—has defined and used the following corporate values for hiring new employees (Fig. 5.10).

These values have been defined at an early point of time as the founders believed that success necessarily requires a high commitment from each employee to all three values. Two of the three values have been further broken down and should be explained next.

For the entrepreneurial value, we use the analogy of an entrepreneur being an athlete as we believe this would be the most suitable analogy. In

Our Mindset & Culture

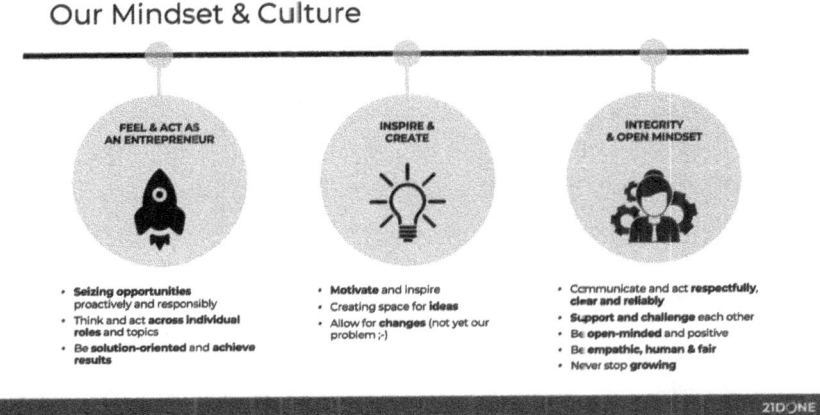

Fig. 5.10 Values of 21done's corporate culture

fact, we have been inspired by Pascal Finette (2014), who compares an entrepreneurs' life with an athlete: "We all know how much blood, sweat and tears goes into an athlete's performance at the Olympic games. She trained for years, spent every spare minute refining her technique, doing one more round on the track, pushing herself even further, staying the extra time when everyone else was having a good time. And yet entrepreneurs think it is easy. That it is all about luck and the right idea at the right time in the right place. It is not.

Entrepreneurship is about dedication. Effort. Perseverance. Doing the work. Not giving up. Grinding it out. Putting in the extra hour. We are the athletes of the business world. Our start-up is Olympia". Based on this analogy, the following principles were defined to stimulate an entrepreneurial culture (Fig. 5.11):

The principles are briefly described as follow:

1. We focus to achieve something great: As an athlete would focus on the next championship, a start-up's employees need to focus on the necessary steps to realise the start-up's vision. Every distraction from this needs to be avoided until the start-up becomes stable in terms of company structure and market success.

Fig. 5.11 Principles to stimulate an entrepreneurial culture at 21done

2. We define subgoals and deadline: An athlete who wants to win, e.g. the Olympic games must not win all competitions before the big event. But it must progress towards the event and reach defined milestones to top perform when it counts.
3. We are ambitious: To be able to compete with incumbents in a certain industry requires strong progress on a daily, weekly, and monthly basis. The bigger vision will help to execute the many little steps each day and go the extra mile while employees of an incumbent may feel too confident and work with less passion.
4. We challenge and coach each other: Being coached and challenged is very important to stay motivated and to ensure that the right actions are taken on an ongoing basis.
5. We are persistent: Ambitious people operate fast as time is a critical variable. Failure will occur on an ongoing basis. And that is ok. Learning from these and not losing enthusiasm is key, or as Winston Churchill said: "Success is going from failure to failure without loss of enthusiasm".

Regarding the third value of 21done's corporate culture (integrity and open mindset), we are in line with the IMPACT formula (Founder Institute, 2021):

1. Integrity—Be honest in all of your dealings and treat people fairly as you honor your commitments in pursuit of your mission.
2. Mission—Articulate a large vision to make the world better and make it your mission to achieve that vision.
3. Pay it Forward—Proactively help others to succeed with their vision by sharing the wisdom from your failures and successes.
4. Adaptable—Learn and improve the business continuously over time in the pursuit of your vision.
5. Collaborative—Work with others and practice inclusion across age, gender, and race to realise your vision.
6. Transparency—Foster a culture that openly shares all reasonable operational details of your business to develop your vision.

In terms of implementation of these values, the founders first wrote these down, communicated them to employees and used the same in the hiring process. A next step was to also base leadership payment on the perceived living of these values.

Implementation of corporate values, however has not been as straightforward as described above. Firstly, it is not easy to identify the values a new person brings in. Secondly, things like an open mindset are good pre-requisites, but the relevant input for learning and being inspired must be organised and often financed. Thirdly, running and working for a start-up is a very stressful thing as the start-up constantly operates with few resources but needs to be ambitious at the same time. Therefore, stress can be detrimental to make good values come alive. Building and sustaining a corporate culture as the exemplary one sketched above needs constant work and energy. Here, the start-up's world is not different to the real life.

5.3 What?

With the "Why" and "How" in place, companies need to keep those in mind as they proceed to define the "What" which refers to experience elements. Since experience elements can include a wide spectrum of things from product, services, prices to touchpoints, this chapter serves to categorise the experience elements into two main groups: customer solutions and go-to-market (G2M) approach.

5.3.1 Customer Solution

Solutions can take many forms: online vs. offline, B2B vs. B2C, service vs. product, priced vs. non-priced. With a focus on start-ups in today's digital times, focus is placed on digital platform solutions as well as the different touchpoints used before, during, and after its usage. First, the platform framework in Fig. 5.12 is a good structure to frame the various elements which companies need to take into consideration during the ideation process.

It is important to note that companies should employ the framework in combination with the customer journey map to understand the context and importance of the different interactions at various phases of the customer journey and leverage on the insights gathered about their pain and gain points to enhance the customer journey and experience.

The platform framework contains the elements customer added values, pricing, interaction objects and design elements. Firstly, the

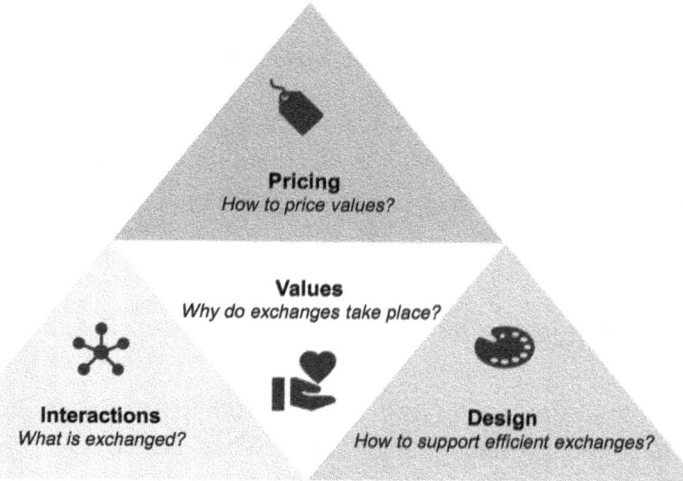

Fig. 5.12 The platform framework

5 Outside-In: Defining the CX-Centric Business DNA—The Why...

	Airbnb	Uber	Amazon
Added value for consumers	• Filters offer fast findability of suitable accommodations • User reviews help with the rental decision	• Info about available rides and drivers • Display of estimated prices and trip duration	• Extensive and easily available assortment • Fast delivery and transparency regarding the delivery status
Added value for producers	• Access to travellers worldwide • AI-based price proposals for accommodation • Uncomplicated booking process	• Access to consumers in a particular city • Simple driver registration • Simple transactions • Good planning capability due to bookings made in advance	• Access to buyers worldwide • Uncomplicated purchase process
Added value for both	• Curation system that connects the right customers with the right producers quickly and easily	• Flat rate car insurance	• Customer reviews help customers and producers

Fig. 5.13 Added value of platform companies (adapted from Choudary et al., 2016)

customer-added values should be worked out since they influence all other framework elements. The first question to ask is: who is the customer? In the case of a neutral aggregator of supply and demand (e.g. Airbnb), there are two types of customers or parties: the consumer as well as the producer. The producer is the one who sets the supply. In the case of Airbnb, this is the apartment owner who offers his apartment. For both parties, value-added services must be offered so that they use the platform and pay for selected services. Figure 5.13 shows examples of the added value that the platform companies Airbnb, Uber, and Amazon offer producers and consumers.

Price and demand are often inversely proportional. When defining the *pricing strategy*, companies need to find a spot that not only generates their desired profit level but which ensures that customer added values are minimally reduced in order to enable a network effect that is highly dependent on the quantity sold. The choice of the added values to be priced must therefore be considered very carefully. The two classic options for pricing are:

- Pricing of *transactions*: e.g. pricing when an Uber ride materialises.
- Pricing of *flat-rate access* to core users or particularly relevant services: e.g. Spotify premium offers ad-free music streaming, and Amazon Prime enables free shipping.

Interaction objects represent the central control instruments for generating added value on the platform. A basic distinction can be made between currency, information, and product/service objects, each of which is used or exchanged on a platform.

- *Currency objects* can be monetary and non-monetary. Non-monetary currencies are, for example likes or written customer reviews. Both forms can provide access to platform offerings in the form of products and services.
- *Relevant information* is required to enable the effective matching of provider and demander. In a higher-level sense, they represent the design elements to be described below. Examples of relevant information are the displayed driver information at Uber or the search results at Google or eBay.
- The result of the information exchange is the exchange of *products and services* or value units. This exchange can take place on the platform (e.g. Facebook, YouTube) or off the platform (e.g. Uber, eBay).

Design elements are relevant for an efficient exchange of interaction objects. Three elements can be distinguished here:

- *Filters*: Filters are a technological megatrend. They enable the successful networking of platform users by allowing the right products or services to meet the right consumers in an efficient manner. Examples include price, apartment size, and location filters on Airbnb.
- *Feedback loop*: User feedback makes future interactions more efficient. Ratings on YouTube and Airbnb or Wikipedia's correction system are some examples. The latter beats the curators of the Encyclopedia Britannica.
- *Barrier reduction*: Platform providers provide an infrastructure to simplify the generation of added value. For example, they offer opportuni-

ties for collaboration (e.g. exchanging messages at Airbnb) or the reduction of transaction costs through flat-rate product insurance (such as in car sharing).

Based on the platform framework, it is clear that a platform (and also a single touchpoint) cannot be separated from the processes that run on it. A price filter, for example is a static element for offering the customer personalised offers in a dynamic way. If the customer responds to one of these offers, a purchase process has been initiated. This buying process can be even more efficient and effective if the platform proactively offers user data-based recommendations in an automated manner, independent of filter settings. By employing this framework, companies can take on a systematic and comprehensive approach for ideation.

The platform framework has first provided a comprehensive overview of the different components which companies need to take into consideration when defining a solution. Following that, the touchpoint template is important for companies to design their individual touchpoints as it encourages an in-depth analysis of each touchpoint which is important for designing the customer journey the start-up wants to accomplish.

The touchpoint template in Fig. 5.14 provides a structure for companies to model various micro-experiences, which will eventually add up to form the macro-experience. It serves as a checklist to help companies identify potential gaps which are important for effective implementation but may have been overlooked. An example of an online payment touchpoint is illustrated in the template in Fig. 5.14. As shown on the template, the desired results and experiences that the customer experiences when interacting with the touchpoint elements are to be defined first. The touchpoint elements themselves are to be worked out in step two, the concrete interaction with them in step three. In the fourth step, companies need to define the means and persons required to make the results mentioned in step one possible. Step five pays into the concept of customer engagement (Brodie et al., 2011), which is increasingly important in many respects, by explicitly describing the ways in which customers can be co-creators in the development and optimisation of experience elements. Step six in the design template connects the user to the template of the next touchpoint—in this case, the next web page. The

Touchpoint-Template

Example: Online Payment

I. **Desired Results**	II. **Experience Elements**	III. **Interactions**
What do you want the customer to experience?	What are the key elements of this touchpoint?	How do interactions take place?
• Customers should feel safe	• Payment options	• Drop-down menu to select the payment option.
• Customer should be able to pay easily	• Clear information (how much?, for what? …)	• Chatbot pops up if customer stays interactive longer
• Customers should be able to choose their payment preference	• Safety and help information	

IV. **Contributors**	V. **Co-Creation**	VI. **Transfer**
Who and what make the results possible?	What will customers do?	How does the customer get to the next touchpoint?
• CX manager who implements customer needs	• Selection of payment option	• Customer is directed to the next web page where payment success is confirmed.
• UX designer for smooth interaction with digital side	• If necessary, saving the payment information for the next transaction	• End of the purchase transaction
• IT for data transfer etc.	• …	

Fig. 5.14 The touchpoint template (adapted from Rossman & Duerden, 2019)

sequence of touchpoints used individually one after the other by the customer in the context of a purchase results in the customer journey. This chaining enables the *orchestration* of experience elements.

5.3.2 Go-to-Market Approach

With the business and brand model defined in the earlier chapters, the missing piece to completing the go-to-market approach is the marketing and sales plan. With an increasing shift to the digital environment, digital marketing communication gains prominence and will hence be covered in this chapter. This form of communication should be given special attention in digital age. In particular, this chapter will highlight three elements of digital marketing communication that are of overriding importance in conception and implementation:

1. Goals of digital communication
2. Digital content to achieve the objectives, and
3. Implementation or orchestration of digital communication or content (elaborated in Sect. 6.2)

5 Outside-In: Defining the CX-Centric Business DNA—The Why...

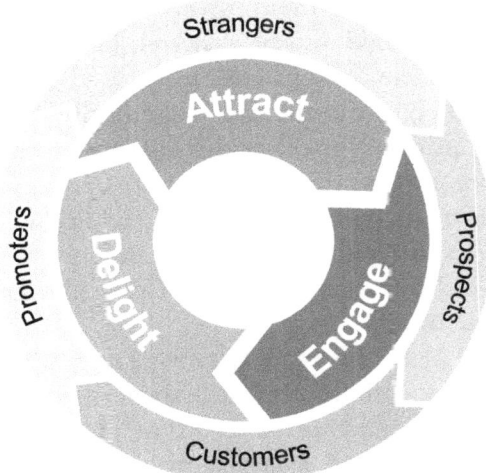

Fig. 5.15 The hubspot marketing flywheel (adapted from Hubspot, 2021)

In the context of marketing, the Flywheel model (see Fig. 5.15) has also been adapted by HubSpot to provide a framework for companies to plan their marketing and sales strategy with specific objectives. As mentioned in Sect. 5.2.1, the Flywheel leverages on the belief that customers are the key to driving growth. In the case of marketing, the core idea is that customers should be attracted, engaged, and delighted through the customer experience with the aim of converting them into brand advocates. In addition, it is recommended that the Flywheel model is used in conjunction with the customer journey to identify the touchpoints and channels where customers experience various needs, emotions, and pain points to help companies decide on the different marketing activities that should take and where they should they place (Hubspot, 2021).

In the attract phase, the objective of the marketing plan is to create awareness around the company's brand, capture potential customers with value-adding content and reduce the obstacles they face when attempting to understand more about the company. It is important to not force the brand on the target customers but to earn their attention through creating attention on the identified customer problem, such that they are drawn to it and willingly show interests in what the company has to offer.

Apart from defining what the company should do to achieve that, the question "where" should also be answered in order to effectively reach them. Here, the identified channels from Sect. 4.1.2 where target customers usually frequent at the first phase of the customer journey can provide useful insights. To achieve this objective, companies can leverage on instruments such as content marketing, search engine optimisation, social media marketing and advertising. In addition, it is also important to define metrics and goals for each stage. Some common metrics for the attract phase includes number of leads collected, impressions and click rates (Hubspot, 2021).

In the engage phase, the key is to provide users with the relevant product or service information to convince them that the company or brand is better than the competitors and to simplify the path to purchase for users. Since customers will always be making comparisons between different competitive options, the company which is able to engage with customers and explain its solution fit to the customer problem will gain a competitive edge. Some tools include marketing automation, customer reviews, customer service, lead nurturing and personalisation of website and email. Common metrics for the engage phase include email open rate, bounce rate, click rate and conversion rate (Hubspot, 2021).

In the delight phase, customers should be supported and empowered to fulfil their jobs-to-be-done such that they have a good experience and are willing to promote the brand to their own network. This phase does not only include the purchase stage but also the stages that proceed. This means that it is important for companies to continually engage with their customers even after purchase and to take on a proactive stance towards understanding their experience with the product or service. Useful tools to use to delight include proactive customer service, feedback surveys and loyalty programmes. Common metrics for the delight phase include customer satisfaction, NPS, retention rates, revenue growth and customer lifetime value.

The metrics and goals used in the three phases should be carefully defined as they can have impacts on the long-term success of the company. Metrics can be differentiated according to three different criteria: the criteria of volume, quality, and value (see Fig. 5.16).

5 Outside-In: Defining the CX-Centric Business DNA—The Why...

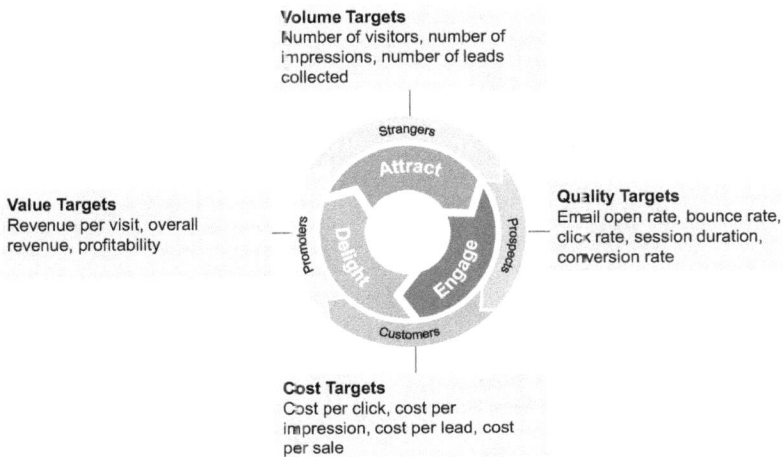

Fig. 5.16 Volume, quality, value, and cost targets of digital communication tools (adapted from Chaffey and Ellis-Chadwick, 2019, p.157)

Volume targets are only of limited relevance to corporate success, as they do not make any statements about website quality or conversion in terms of value. An unsatisfied website user who immediately leaves the site pays into the volume goal, but not into higher value goals such as revenue conversion. In contrast, quality goals such as a low bounce rate as well as a high dwell time can contribute more strongly to directly revenue-relevant actions (e.g. conversion in the e-commerce store) or indirectly revenue-relevant actions (e.g. app download, positive digital customer rating, engagement) being performed on a digital page. In general, volume targets are particularly important in the Attract phase, quality targets are pertinent for the Engage phase, while value targets are most relevant in the Delight phase. Lastly, cost targets (e.g. cost per click) should also be taken into consideration, especially for start-ups due to limited initial capital.

Depending on the defined goals, the next step is to plan and develop the content to support achievement of the goals. Figure 5.17 can serve as content inspiration for various marketing purposes. For instance, quick and fun content such as quizzes and infographics are effective for

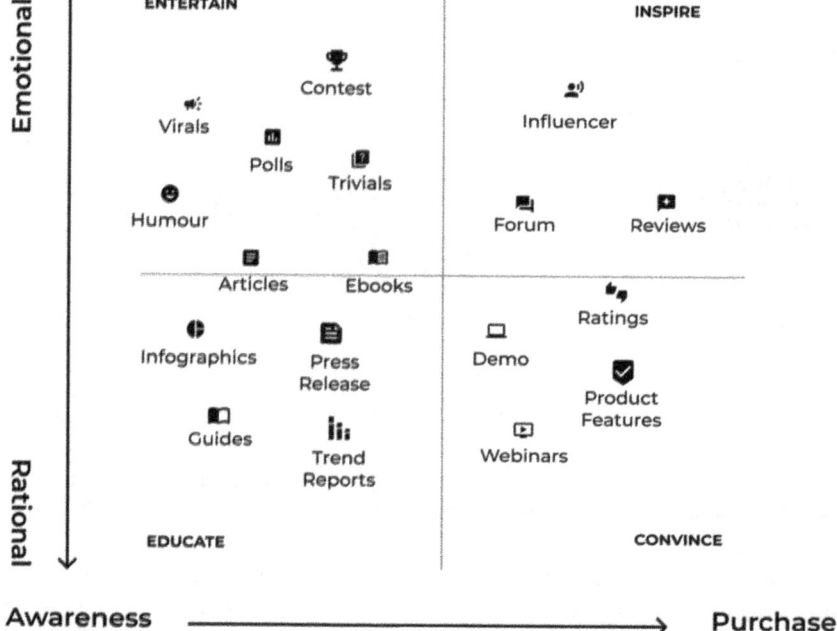

Fig. 5.17 Content types along degree of emotion and customer journey (adapted from Smart Insights, 2014)

attracting attention to create awareness, while convincing content such as reviews and demos are useful for moving users towards the purchase decision. The content types are also placed on an emotional spectrum, from emotional to rational, to allow for the creation of varied experiences which can be used for different target customers and circumstances.

In addition, the following aspects, among others, must be taken into account in the concrete design of the content:

1. *Shareability:* In digital times, shareable content is especially important. This is because communication messages can spread quickly and nationwide in the digital space—although this naturally also applies to content that is perceived negatively!

2. *Fit:* The content must fit the company, target group, and medium. For example younger users on Snapchat expect significantly "hipper"and shorter posts than users of the company's website or Instagram account.
3. *Headline:* Across all media, it is important to pay close attention to the respective headline when creating content. As the headline of a website article is exposed and linked through different channels such as Google search results, subject line of an email or Instagram post, it is particularly relevant for the attention and behaviour of the user.

"On average, five times as many people read the headline as they read the body copy. When you have written your headline, you have spent eighty cents out of your dollar". (David Ogilvy 2014). The following are seven tips (including examples) for writing an attention-generating and action-oriented headline:

1. Integrate numbers (at the beginning)—"7 ways to happiness"!
2. Use phrase "How to"—"How to become a digital expert in one week"!
3. Address known errors—"Customer Churn? Doesn't have to be anymore thanks to Data Science"!
4. Ask questions—"Who has the best chance of winning the world title"?
5. Use short, concise headlines—"Google typically shows the first 50–60 characters".
6. Add photos—They generate attention and should reflect the content appropriately.
7. Use best practices—"Top 3 top tools to optimise your customer journey".

Before diving into the ideation of experience elements, this chapter will provide a recap of the key dimensions influencing customer experience, which companies should keep in mind during the experience elements ideation process. These dimensions, if effectively managed, can lead to good customer experiences. As such, it is worthwhile for companies to keep these different aspects in mind while designing experience elements. In general, these models converge to the following aspects: trust, ease of use, service, emotions, social influence and physical environment (Havir, 2017).

1. Trust is an important component when it comes to designing experience elements. It relates to the reliability of the service or product, its availability and fulfilment as well as security and privacy of user data. For instance, companies can introduce instruments such as money-back guarantee, effective inventory management and customer support systems.
2. Ease of use which could manifest through the user interface, efficiency and whether the customer can successfully achieve his outcome, should also be considered, e.g. UX-optimised website flow, clear path to purchase and easy checkout.
3. Companies need to also design superior customer service in order to effectively support customer needs and engage with them, e.g. well-trained customer service personnel who are able to accurately and promptly answer the enquiries of customers.
4. It is also important that experience elements are designed to evoke positive emotions as this can strongly influence the memorability and overall feelings towards the brand or company. In general, companies should strive to bring customers positive emotions such as happiness, appreciation, and peace of mind. Following that, experience elements should also be designed to leverage on the social influence of consumers, e.g. social reviews, user-generated content and referral marketing. Last but not least, the environment in which the customer makes his purchase is also a crucial influence on the customer experience, and this relates to the website design and retail atmosphere. With a broad overview of the "What" in mind, the next chapter will take a deeper dive into the process of ideating to the implementation of experience elements.

5.3.3 Ideation Techniques for Customer Solutions and G2M Strategy

This chapter continues to answer the question "What?" and more in the direction of "What Exactly?". After the corporate DNA as well as the brand and customer strategy have been developed on the basis of the desired experiences that a customer should have in his interaction with the company, the company is well equipped to design experience elements that customers will perceive and interact with. These elements ultimately represent the concrete potential for creating the desired customer experiences, which are intended to turn the customer into a first and subsequent buyer and, ideally, into an advocator of the company.

Everything begins with an idea, so does an experience element. Ideation is a core process in facilitating the discovery of solutions to customer problems, and potential optimisations to enhancing customer experience. As such, this chapter will cover various ideation techniques which companies can use to generate new ideas and solutions for not only the identified customer problems but also process, product and service designs.

Brainstorming One of the best-known creativity methods in business practice is brainstorming due to its wide range of applications. It can be used in product and service development as well as, for example in the design of business models, touchpoints and communication measures. The basic idea of brainstorming is to allow as many ideas as possible within a group of selected experts by thinking aloud (Osborn, 1963; Vahs & Brem, 2015). The size of the group should be between five and eight people, and the people should come from as many different areas as possible (e.g. marketing, sales, service, innovation, business development, IT). The moderator has a particularly important role to play, as he must ensure the following brainstorming rules (Kreutzer, 2019):

- Any idea is welcome.
- The more impulsive and passionate an idea is, the better.
- Criticism is forbidden.
- Free associations in relation to the ideas of others are desired ("Thinking ahead").

A brainstorming session should not be longer than 30–45 min. Otherwise, fatigue can set in, hindering impulsivity. It is also important that the area in which ideas are searched for is clearly defined. E.g. the search area "product innovations for the B2C segment in Western Europe" can be delineated even more clearly. Figure 5.18 shows one of the many structuring options as an example.

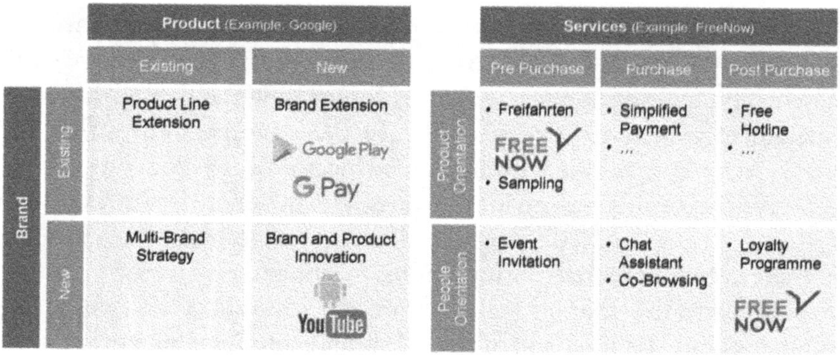

Fig. 5.18 Sample structure for a product or service brainstorming session (adapted from Kreutzer & Land, 2017, p.57)

The brainstorming method can be used in isolation or also in the context of the design thinking approach, which is more holistic in terms of the innovation process. The holistic nature of the design thinking approach is due, among other things, to the fact that it does not provide only one explicit process step for the original generation of ideas (Ideation phase in Fig. 5.19), in which the brainstorming method could be integrated. Instead, the problem is derived intensively beforehand in the "Define phase" on the basis of the "Empathise phase", which is geared to a deep understanding of the customer. Likewise, process steps for rapid development ("Prototyping"), early testing ("Testing") and implementation ("Implementation") of the solution are explicitly provided.

Design Thinking Design Thinking is a non-linear and iterative user-centric approach to understand the user, challenge assumptions, and redefine problems with the intention to identify alternative solutions that are less obvious with an initial level of understanding (Dam and Teo 2020). The three basic principles of process, space, and team of Design Thinking have led to its popularity as a corporate practice and the belief that "people from different disciplines [team] should work together in an environment [space] that promotes creativity, jointly develop an issue, consider people's needs and motivations, and then develop concepts that are tested multiple times [process]" (M.I.T., 2018). The process (see

5 Outside-In: Defining the CX-Centric Business DNA—The Why...

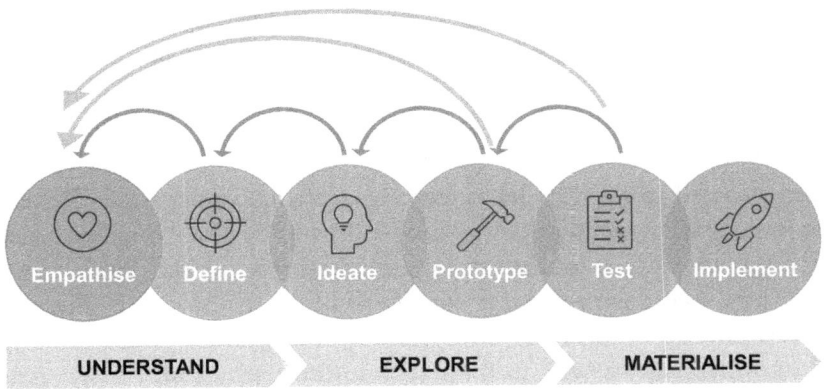

Fig. 5.19 The design thinking process (adapted from Nielsen Norman Group, 2016)

Fig. 5.19) contains six steps: empathise, define, ideate, prototype, test, and implement. It should be noted that the steps are not strictly in order and can be revisited whenever necessary.

Empathise The first step of the process involves developing an empathetic understanding of the customer problem which a company aims to solve. The tools in Sect. 4.1.2, e.g. empathy map, customer interviews and customer journey map, serve to help companies achieve an in-depth understanding of the problems from the perspective of the customer (Gibbons, 2016).

Define The next step of the process is to define the core problem based on the insights gathered from the first step. The outcome of this step is a customer-oriented problem statement. A useful template to generate a comprehensive customer problem statement is as follows:

I am *(characteristics of customers)*, trying to *(jobs-to-be-done: what are they trying to achieve?)*, but *(problems faced: what challenges do they face?)* because *(root cause: what is the underlying cause of the problem?)* which makes me feel *(emotions: how are the customers emotionally affected as a result?)*

By employing this structure, companies are able to gain a holistic overview of the customer problem and solve the problem from a multitude of perspectives.

Ideate With a well-defined customer problem statement, companies can then proceed to generate ideas targeted at the customer need. There are various ideation techniques that can be used to facilitate the idea generation process such as brainstorming (as mentioned earlier), brainwriting, how-how technique and more which will be explained later in this chapter. At the end of this stage, companies should arrive at various plausible ideas which can be used to solve the customer problem. At that point, companies can begin an early round of idea testing with potential customers to gain initial insights on customer perception and acceptance of the idea. It is important to note that companies with ideas that require a prototype to illustrate the idea can begin testing after the next step: prototype.

Prototype The prototyping phase is where ideas become tangible, and companies can get overly excited. Hence, it is crucial to understand that prototypes are intended to provide early and approximately realistic insights in the testing phase without wasting resources and should be developed in a low cost and scaled-down manner. Solutions should be implemented within the prototypes one by one, investigated and either accepted, refined, or rejected based on the user experience.

Test With the prototype developed, companies can use it to test the idea with the employees and potential customers. Based on user feedback on the prototype, companies can refine the product and re-test to see if the enhancements have improved the customer experience. Testing can also take place using alternative prototypes. A/B testing in particular has enjoyed great popularity for many years with regards to testing smaller features and incremental changes, especially in the digital space. It will therefore be described in more detail in Sect. 6.1.2. It is important to note that the process is non-linear, e.g. user feedback from the testing phase can lead companies to revisit or rethink the customer problem statement defined in stage X and rework the process from that there.

Implement After several rounds of iterations, the process gives rise to a thoroughly tested and well-defined idea that is ready for implementation. At this stage, companies need to ensure that their solution idea transforms into a real product or feature which customers can use to solve their problem. At this point, the design thinking process continues as the developed product is regularly tested and refined to better meet user needs. In addition, the process continues with newly defined customer problems and will be ongoing as long as the production is in operation.

Figure 5.20 shows the exemplary outcomes of the ideation, prototyping, and development process in the context of developing a mobile website. Companies intending to develop a mobile site begin the ideation process with a sketch or wireframe to roughly illustrate the idea in a visual way. Once it is tested and proven to hold potential, the company then proceeds to develop an interactive prototype, also known as mock-ups, which allows users to experience the product and provide feedback on the experience. Once the prototype has undergone several rounds of refinement and testing, the company can then proceed to developing the real product.

At this point, it may seem that the stages mimic the customer experience framework. However, it is important to note that the design thinking process takes a more specific approach and helps companies focus on a single problem each time.

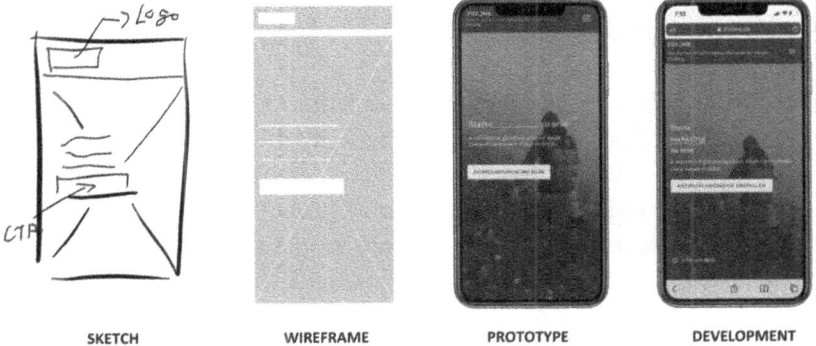

SKETCH   WIREFRAME   PROTOTYPE   DEVELOPMENT

Fig. 5.20 Prototyping methods in the context of website creation (adapted from Traynham, 2019)

As a summary, the design thinking approach

- Combines a high level of customer orientation (e.g. with the help of the Empathise and Test phases or the interdisciplinary teams) with an entrepreneurial focus on goals (e.g. with the help of the Define and Prototype phases).
- Ensures that new findings from later phases are integrated and used in previous phases by means of iterations or the recurring passage through various work steps.
- Incorporates a philosophy of "fail, but fail fast!", which encourages high-speed experimental innovation.

6-3-5 Brainwriting The 6-3-5 brainwriting method is a form of brainstorming to generate a huge number of ideas within a short amount of time of 30 min. A complete round of brainwriting includes a group of six participants, who facilitated by a moderator, are required to note three new ideas down on a worksheet within 5 min. After 5 min, each participant swaps their worksheet with another team member and notes down another three ideas, which could either build on the previous idea or be completely new. This repeats until each worksheet is filled with the contributions of all six members, and the outcome is 108 ideas in 30 min (Schröer et al., 2010). This method leverages on the different perspectives and experiences of participants to contribute their ideas as well as to add to others' ideas, creating a sizeable number of ideas which the team can sift through and explore in detail.

How-How Diagram The how-how is a simple but effective method for generating practical solutions to an identified problem by a repeated questioning of "How?". Participants first ask, "how can the identified problem be solved?" and come up with as many answers as possible to this question. Next, they look at the answers generated in the first round and ask "how?" and again provide as many as ideas as possible. This process then repeats until no additional answers can be provided or until a practical solution has been generated. The team can then analyse the solutions generated and perform a prioritisation analysis. The outcome is

	Description	Example
Substitute	Ideas should be broken down into individual components to check if anything can be substituted with an alternative	A car-sharing company like Uber has substituted company owned cars with private hires.
Combine	Existing ideas can be merged to complement flaws or to increase total value	WeChat is not simply a messaging platform but a social media channel, and an online booking and payment platform, making it the single go-to app for the Chinese users.
Adapt	An existing idea can be adapted to meet a different need	iTunes used to be a music purchase app but has become a music streaming app
Modify/Magnify	The quality of an object can be changed, or features can be magnified to improve added value	Spotify and Netflix offer subscription-based pricing model which allow them to increase the frequency of payment and cash flow predictability
Put to other use	Existing ideas can be put to better uses	The concept of video conferencing has been put into the medical industry to provide telemedicine services
Eliminate	Products, services and processes can be analysed to check for features or stages to be eliminated	Digital banks, such as N26, has eliminated the need for physical processes and outlets by digitizing processes.
Reverse	Ideas can be analysed in a different manner in terms of its product, service and process delivery	Amazon has reversed the process of returns by providing free return labels for product returns to increase the likelihood of purchase

Fig. 5.21 SCAMPER techniques and examples

a hierarchical tree structure that provides a solution break-down targeted at the initial problem (Serrat, 2017a).

SCAMPER The SCAMPER technique is a consolidation of nine principal ways to manipulate a subject to give rise to new and innovative ideas. The mnemonic SCAMPER stands for substitute, combine, adapt, modify/magnify/minimise, put to other uses, eliminate, and rearrange. To employ the SCAMPER technique, companies can put their ideas under the seven different context, as illustrated in Fig. 5.21 (Serrat, 2017b).

References

Bezos, J. (2001). *The Amazon flywheel in Peppler (2019) The Amazing flywheel effe*ct. Accessed July 15, 2021, from https://medium.com/swlh/the-amazing-flywheel-effect-80a0a21a5ea7

Breton, G. (2020). *21 Real life examples of successful affiliate marketing websites in 2021*. Accessed July 26, 2021, from https://www.authorityhacker.com/successful-affiliate-websites-examples/

Brodie, R. J., Hollebeek, L., Juric, B., & Ilic, A. (2011). Customer engagement: Conceptual domain, fundamental propositions, and implications for research. *Journal of Service Research, 17*, 1–20.

Bruhn, M. (2018). *Communication policy: Systematic use of communication for companies.* Vahlen.

Chaffey, D., & Ellis-Chadwick, F. (2019). *Digital marketing.*

Comparably. (2021). *Starbucks Awards.* Accessed June 20, 2021, from https://www.comparably.com/companies/starbucks/awards

Cothran, H. M., & Wysocki, A. F. (2005). *Developing SMART goals for your organization.* University of Florida. IFAS Extension.

Cuofano, G. (2021). *Amazon flywheel: Amazon virtuous cycle in a nutshell.* Accessed July 27, 2021, from https://fourweekmba.com/amazon-flywheel/

Cuofano, G. (2020a). *Business models.* Accessed June 24, 2021, from https://fourweekmba.com/what-is-a-business-model/

Cuofano, G. (2020b). *What is the cost structure of a business model and why it matters.* Accessed July 26, 2021, from https://fourweekmba.com/cost-structure-business-model/

Dam, R. F., & Teo, Y. S. (2020). What is Design Thinking and Why Is It So Popular. Accessed 29 July 2021, from https://www.interactiondesign.org/literature/article/what-is-design-thinking-and-why-is-it-so-popular

Darbi, W. P. K. (2012). Mission and vision statements and their potential impact on employee behaviour and attitudes: The case study of a public but profit oriented tertiary institution. *International Journal of Business and Social Sciences., 3*(14).

Esch, F. (2017). *Strategie und Technik der Markenführung* (4th ed.). Vahlen.

ESCH. (n.d.). *Markensteuerrad.* Accessed July 30, 2021, from https://www.esch-brand.com/glossar/markensteuerrad/

Founder Institute. (2018). *The 10 most popular startup revenue models.* Accessed July 29, 2021, from https://fi.co/insight/the-10-most-popular-startup-revenue-models

Founder Institute. (2021). http://www.fi.co/

Gibbons, S. (2016). *Design thinking 101.* Nielsen Norman Group. Accessed July 29, 2021, from https://www.nngroup.com/articles/design-thinking/

Havir, D. (2017). A comparison of the approaches to customer experience analysis. *Economics and Business, 31.* https://doi.org/10.1515/eb-2017-0020

Hubspot. (2021). *The flywheel.* Accessed August 1, 2021, from https://www.hubspot.com/flywheel

Ikea. (2021). *Vision, culture and values*. Accessed July 22, 2021, from https://ikea.jobs.cz/en/vision-culture-and-values/

Inpowercoaching. (2019). *Why collaboration is the key to success in business*. Accessed September 28, 2021, from https://inpowercoaching.com/why-collaboration-is-the-key-to-success-in-business/

Jeffries, I. (2018). *How to fill in a business model canvas*. Accessed July 26, 2021, from https://isaacjeffries.com/blog/2018/9/8/how-to-fill-in-a-business-model-canvas

Kapferer, J. N. (2009). *Kapferer's Brand-Identity Prism Model*. European Institute for Brand Management.

Kapferer J N (2012). The new strategic brand management: Advanced insights and strategic thinking.

Keeley, L., Pikkel, R., Quinn, B., & Walters, H. (2013). *Ten types of innovation*. Wiley.

Keiningham, T. L., Aksoy, L., Bruce, H., Cadet, F., Clennell, N., Hodgkinson, I. R., & Kearney, T. (2020). Customer experience driven business model innovation. *Journal of Business Research, 116*, 431–440. https://doi.org/10.1016/j.jbusres.2019.08.003

Kreutzer, R. (2019). *Toolbox for marketing and management*. Springer.

Kreutzer, R., & Land, K. H. (2017). *Digitale Markenführung: Digital Branding im Zeitalter des digitalen Darwinismus*. Springer Gabler.

Kylliäinen, J. (2019). *Types of Innovation – The Ultimate Guide with Definitions and Examples*. Accessed 7 August 2021, from https://www.viima.com/blog/types-of-innovation#ten-types-of-innovation

Maurya, A. (2010). *Lean canvas*. Accessed July 20, 2021, from https://bmtoolbox.net/tools/lean-canvas/

Meyer, C., & Schwager, A. (2007). Understanding customer experience. *Harvard Business Review*. https://idcexed.com/wp-content/uploads/2021/01/Understanding_Customer_Experience.pdf

M.I.T. World. (2018). *Innovation through design thinking, video of talk by Tim Brown at Massachusetts Institute of Technology*. Accessed July 20, 2021, from https://techtv.mit.edu/videos/16098-innovation-through-design-thinking

Nesvit, A. (2021). *TOP 7 online marketplace revenue models in 2020*. Accessed July 26, 2021, from https://sloboda-studio.com/blog/online-marketplace-revenue-models/

Nielsen Norman Group. (2016). *Design thinking 101*. Nielsen Norman Group. Accessed July 29, 2021, from https://www.nngroup.com/articles/design-thinking/

Nugno. (2019). *What is the brand identity prism?* Accessed August 10, 2021, from https://medium.com/@bynugno/what-is-the-brand-identity-prism-5ae71e43ab4a

Ogilvy, D. (2004). *Confessions of an Advertising Man.* Southbank. London.

Ogilvy, D. (2014). *Excerpt from 'Confessions of an Advertising Man'.* Accessed September 12, 2021, from https://www.campaignlive.co.uk/article/excerpt-confessions-advertising-man/996114

O'Malley, P. (2020). *Discover the 4 types of minimum viable product.* Accessed July 27, 2021, from https://openclassrooms.com/en/courses/4544561-learn-about-lean-startup/4703206-discover-the-4-types-of-minimum-viable-product

Osborn, A. (1963). *Applied imagination.* Charles Scribner's Son.

Osterwalder, A., & Pigneur, Y. (2010). *Business model generation.* Wiley.

Choudary, S., Alstyne, M. W., & Parker, G. G. (2016). *Platform revolution: How networked markets are transforming the economy—and how to make them work for you.*

Finette, P. (2014). *The olympic deception.* Accessed September 25, 2021, from https://read.theheretic.org/the-olympic-deception-71f1586398a7

Rossman, J. R., & Duerden, M. D. (2019). *Designing experiences.* Columbia University Press. ProQuest Ebook Central, Accessed July 15, 2021, from https://ebookcentral.proquest.com/lib/brand-university/detail.action?docID=5613936

Schmitt, B. H., & Rogers, D. L. (2008). *Handbook on brand and experience management.* Edward Elgar.

Schröer, B., Kain, A., & Lindemann, U. (2010). *Supporting creativity in conceptual design: Method 635-extended.*

Serrat, O. (2017a). *The five whys technique.* https://doi.org/10.1007/978-981-10-0983-9_32.

Serrat, O. (2017b). *The SCAMPER technique.* https://doi.org/10.1007/978-981-10-0983-9_33.

Sinek, S. (2009). *Start with why: How great leaders inspire everyone to take action.* Portfolio.

Skowron, M. (2020). *Lean canvas vs business model canvas: Which should you choose?* Accessed August 2, 2021, from https://uigstudio.com/insights/lean-canvas-vs-business-model-canvas-which-should-you-choose

Smart Insights: The Content Marketing Matrix. (2014). Accessed July 25, 2021, from https://www.smartinsights.com/content-management/content-marketing-strategy/the-content-marketing-matrix-new-infographic/

Starbucks. (2015). *Starbucks mission and values*. Accessed June 20, 2021, from https://stories.starbucks.com/press/2015/starbucks-mission-and-values/

Starbucks. (2021). *Company timeline*. Accessed June 20, 2021, from https://stories.starbucks.com/press/2019/company-timeline/

Stegemann, M. (2021). *Customer journey (Part 2)*. Accessed July 15, 2021, from https://www.youtube.com/watch?v=ogSK0faw064

Strategyzer, A. G. (2019). *The 9 building blocks of the business model canvas*. Accessed July 23, 2021, from https://www.strategyzer.com/expertise/business-models

Strategyzer, A. G. (2020). *Business model canvas*. Accessed July 23, 2021, from https://www.strategyzer.com/bmc_thank_you?submissionGuid=4a8cf307-5f8e-427e-a25c-f2be62250a57

Traynham, D. (2019). Design Roles - UX & UI. Accessed 20 July 2021, from https://artandlogic.com/2019/05/design-roles-ux-ui-3/

Xue, J., Zhou, Z., Zhang, L., & Salman, M. (2020). Do brand competence and warmth always influence purchase intention? The moderating role of gender. *Frontiers in Pyschology, 11*. https://doi.org/10.3389/fpsyg.2020.00248

Vahs, D., & Brem, A. (2015). *Innovation management. From the product idea to successful marketing*. Schäffer-Poeschel.

6

Inside-Out: Testing, Implementation, and Communication of Experience Elements

The final step is to test and implement the developed experience elements at the customer touchpoints along the customer journey.

6.1 Testing

An important building block for creating sustainable products and market success is consistent testing. As mentioned in the earlier chapters, it is important for companies to carry out testing regularly on not only its developed product but also on the preceding ideas and assumptions such as customer problem, initial ideas and prototypes. This is extremely crucial as it has significant influence on the success of the end consumer product and can help companies avoid huge cost wastage as a result of producing products that have no market demand. As the earlier chapters have covered testing for the initial idea, this chapter will cover usability testing and A/B testing.

6.1.1 Usability Testing

The main goal of usability testing is to help companies gather information to improve customer and user experience. Usability testing can help to gain an understanding of target customer's behaviour and preferences, identify problems in product design, to discover opportunities for optimisations. Usability testing exists in various forms and serves to identify user experience on a multitude of variables such as effectiveness, efficiency, and satisfaction.

Moderated Usability Tests One of the most common types of usability testing is moderated usability tests which focus on collecting information on user problems, severity of issues, whether tasks can be carried out successfully, effectively, and efficiently. A moderate usability test is a lab test that involves relatively few representative participants, between five and ten. The test is carried out on a one-to-one basis between a moderator and a participant. The moderator poses questions to the participants and provides them a set of tasks to execute on the product which is being tested. Test participants are asked to think out loud as they perform the test in order to facilitate the understanding of the user's thought process. Since such testing is based on the individual expression of the user, it is sometimes not possible that the user covers every specific variable that the company aims to analyse. As such, it may be helpful to add a survey with quantitative and qualitative aspects to enable a more comprehensive coverage. To facilitate a post-test analysis, a recording of the test with the approval of the participants can prove to be helpful for referencing and deeper analysis (Albert & Tullis, 2013). In general, moderated usability tests are expensive and time-consuming but particularly helpful for identifying and delving deeper into the customers' thoughts and perceptions as moderator and users can go back and forth for clarifications.

Unmoderated Usability Tests Digitisation has made testing more accessible online, providing companies convenient means to collect rich information in a relatively short duration. Typically, unmoderated usability tests are set up in a similar way as moderated usability tests with screening noted that it requires expertise for execution and analysis and specialised equipment. In addition to eye tracking, there are also various tools that measure user emotions and stress through facial expressions, skin conductance and the use of Electroencephalograph (EEG), which can also complement the traditional usability testing methods (Wang et al., 2019). Start-ups that are looking to test the feasibility of their ideas at the beginning should not exhaust too many resources on such an intricate testing method as these tools are relatively expensive, and the initial product and design ideas are likely to undergo drastic changes. Hence, the use of eye tracking is recommended for start-ups and companies which are in a relatively stable phase, where these tools can support for design and product enhancements.

Since these methods each have advantages and disadvantages, the most appropriate test should be selected based on the company's objective as well as time and cost constraints. The planning of a usability test should also take into consideration the following factors: execution location, data type, participant type, and the need for a moderator. A combination of different usability tests will often provide a more comprehensive view of the user experience.

6.1.2 A/B Testing

A/B tests represent an increasingly popular form of market testing for testing smaller scale variations, e.g. colours, copywriting, and visuals. They are aimed primarily at optimising marketing activities such as the sending of emails or a company's website. Due to the mass availability of online data in digital times, this quantitative analysis method is increasingly being used by a large number of large and small companies.

What used to be decided by gut feeling or in qualitative group discussions of the marketing team can nowadays be controlled and optimised on the basis of quantitative analyses (here in the context of A/B testing). Test procedures of inferential statistics are used to distinguish random differences from significant differences between the developed variants and to be able to draw conclusions for a larger population. The test results can be used to identify which variant is the most promising, and thus, for questions, prescribed tasks and follow-up questions, and all user-related information is automatically stored. The test processes are also often recorded to enable testers to also acquire observations that can supplement the recorded behaviour. The advantages of unmoderated usability tests lie in their cost-effectiveness and flexibility to collect high quantities of both quantitative and qualitative data and across geographical barriers, making these an increasingly common and accessible test method. Many online tools such as Userzoom, TrymyUI, and Userlytics are also available to simplify this process for companies. In addition, unmoderated testing also allows for more unbiased opinions as testers do not feel obliged to express their views in a positive way. On the other hand, the downside of such a test type is the inability to probe for explanation and elaboration, which is important in achieving an in-depth analysis of user motivations (Albert & Tullis, 2013).

Surveys An alternative form of usability tests is surveys, which provide companies with the flexibility to gather information on user experience without high costs involved. Many online survey tools provide the option to include visuals and scale questions which would facilitate companies in the collection of information about their prototype, especially on variables such as design appeal, layout, perceived ease of use and use intent. In general, surveys are ideal for product testing, which does not require user interactions and can be a complementary add-on to other usability tests (Albert & Tullis, 2013).

Eye Tracking Due to advancements in technologies, eye tracking has become a popular method in usability testing, which incorporates an additional psychophysiological element to usability analyses. Eye tracking tools leverage on the eye-mind hypothesis, which suggests that visual attention is a gauge for mental attention, i.e. visual attention patterns can provide valuable insights on the cognitive processes of individuals. With its versatility, the method can be applied in a multitude of usability tasks such as advertisements and website viewing and provides user insights, including their dwell time, fixations, duration, and flow sequence, which are important insights for companies in rethinking their solution (Albert & Tullis, 2013). While eye tracking is a highly useful tool, it should be

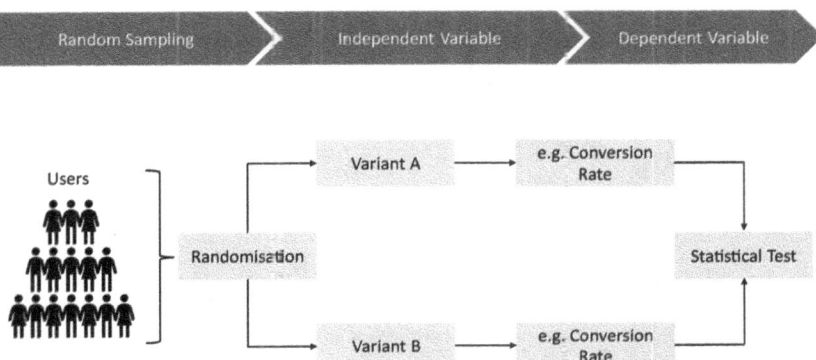

Fig. 6.1 Basic sequence of an A/B test (adapted from Stegemann & Suwelack, 2020)

example the subject line of the newsletter or the online purchase button can be optimised (see Fig. 6.1).

The applicability of A/B tests is extremely broad and covers a wide range of issues in digital marketing. Typical fields of application including exemplary questions and hypotheses are shown in Fig. 6.2 for better illustration.

Incidentally, the different questions can each be assigned to the response in the stimulus-organism-response model (Sect. 5.2.3), since they are each aimed at an observable behaviour. These behaviour-oriented goals each represent conversions and can be divided into two parts as follows:

- Macro-conversions are target variables that can be seen as the desired end result of a consumer behaviour chain and often result in a direct economic effect (e.g. product purchase).
- Micro-conversions, on the other hand, represent preliminary stages in a behavioural chain leading to a macro conversion. In other words, they are intermediate goals along the customer journey. For example bounce rate is defined as leaving a website immediately after calling it up, and reducing this is a goal that can be called a micro-conversion.

Fields of Application	Exemplary Question	Exemplary Hypothesis
Email Marketing	Which subject leads to the highest newsletter open rate?	Mention of an offer is better than "Newsletter [Mon][Year]".
	What is the optimal value of a voucher in terms of ROI?	A discount code of 15 euros will result in a higher ROI than 10 euros.
Website and App	Which image on the landing page is more appealing to visitors?	A more emotional image leads to longer dwell times.
	Where should the possibility to contact be positioned?	Contact in the header is used more than in the footer.
Online Ads	Which ad title is more appealing in Google Ads?	Title XY leads to a higher click-through rate than the current title.
	Should videos be integrated into ads on Facebook?	Videos lead to a higher click-through as well as purchase rate than images.
E-commerce	How should the buy button be designed for optimal conversion?	A green, larger buy button leads to more purchases than the current one.
	What payment options should be available?	Integration of PayPal leads to more purchases than immediate transfers

Fig. 6.2 Overview of typical application fields for A/B tests (adapted from Stegemann & Suwelack, 2020)

In order to be able to draw the right conclusions with regard to these target variables in the context of the A/B test, a systematic approach, as shown in Fig. 6.3, is mandatory. This ideal-typical procedure essentially corresponds to the scientific process when researching a subject. A more in-depth explanation of the individual steps of the process and a description of typical pitfalls, particularly in the statistical execution of A/B tests, will not be provided here. Instead, reference should be made to the literature by Stegemann and Suwelack (2020).

At this point, the core elements of the business have been thoroughly defined and tested and are ready for implementation. However, in the context of start-ups, not many will have the financial resources to pour into product development and marketing, especially if the business requires high-intensity development efforts. As for the companies who managed to collect some initial capital, it is also important to keep investments flowing in to enable the long-term survivability of the company. As such, it is important for companies to consolidate this information into a pitch deck and proceed with funding applications (Sect. 3.2.2).

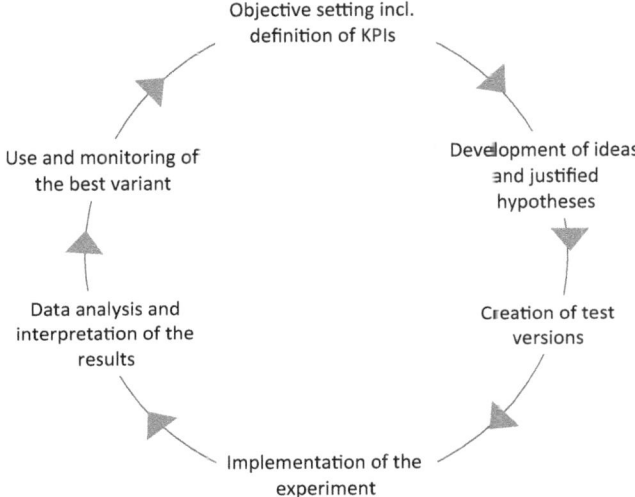

Fig. 6.3 Typical process of A/B testing and multivariate testing (adapted from Stegemann & Suwelack, 2020)

6.2 Implementation

Once the experience elements have been tested and validated, the final step is to make them go live. The implementation of the elements should take place in the sense of orchestration, as consistency (e.g. same look and feel, same information) and coordination (e.g. use of synergies, enabling interactions of different intensity) of touchpoints are highly important. For example not every touchpoint can or should hold emotional, discovery, or even transformational experiences; rather, most experiences will be prosaic and cognitive in nature—as in a concert, where there are more intense and more relaxing phases.

6.2.1 Customer Solutions and Go-to-Market Strategy

Due to the likely limited capital and resources at the beginning stages of start-ups, the implementation of customer solutions should be strategically prioritised in order to keep the business offer lean and focused. Not

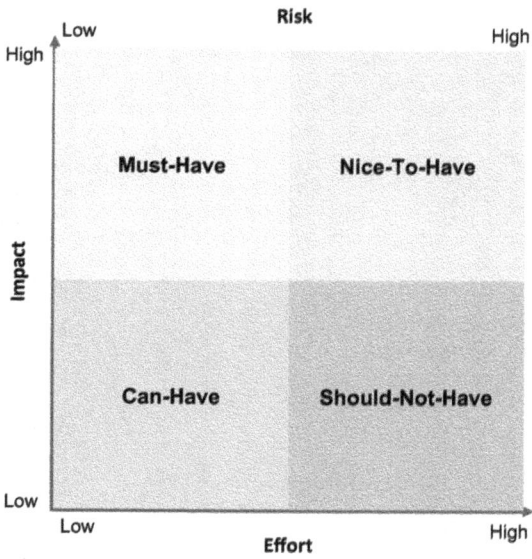

Fig. 6.4 Feature priority matrix (adapted from Valuy, 2020)

all features need to be developed or implemented at one go as the complexity can overwhelm customers who are trying to understand the brand or company in the market, leading to poor customer experience. It is common for companies to want to push for all the ideas they have, but more is not always better. Companies need to prioritise the list of features and ideas they have according to its strategic impact, implementation efforts and risk. The matrix in Fig. 6.4 provides a visual framework for the prioritisation.

Strategic Impact "How is this idea or feature going to add strategic value to the company"? When evaluating an idea, companies need to be able to answer this question. The strategic value here should be connected to the key metrics and goals of the company, which means that the intended impact of this feature helps the company achieve its goals and is measurable. Measurability is important as it can help the company understand if the feature has led to its intended impact. If a feature is expected to have a positive correlation with the company's goal and can be quantified, the feature can be said to have high strategic impact (Valuy, 2020; Yoskovitz, 2011).

Effort Implementation of features requires manpower time and development efforts which can be one of the costliest expenses of a company. Apart from the quantity of resources required for implementation, it is also important to consider the recurrence of the effort, i.e. whether it is a one-time effort or an ongoing effort. For instance, particularly in the technological industry, the software life cost is mainly attributed to the maintenance than development, even though the regular maintenance effort may be seemingly lower than the huge initial development effort (Björklund, 2019). This is due to the fact that the maintenance is an ongoing effort while development is a one-off effort. As such, companies need to weigh the effort required to implement the different features and make the necessary decisions based on limited resources (Valuy, 2020).

Risk The implementation of new features usually comes with some level of risk, whether it is technical risk, acceptance risk or cost risks. For instance, a feature could be too difficult to implement and as a result require too much time, which can lead to opportunity cost on other development areas (Valuy, 2020).

By using the three criteria to evaluate the features, companies can better prioritise their needs and make better use of their resources. Must-have features include low-risk features which solve user problems and should be implemented early. Can-be-done features are low-risk features that demand little effort which also bring about low impact on users. These can be implemented to not waste development efforts and to first understand if customers need the core product. Nice-to-have features are the ones that contain unique solutions but are challenging to implement. These features should be considered for the next implementation to provide added value, but not at the beginning as it can be overly taxing for the company. Last but not least, features which fall under should-not-have are low on strategic impact yet high on risk and effort. As such, it is not wise to implement such features (Valuy, 2020).

Next, in order for such a "concert" or harmonising customer experiences to occur in the first place from the customer's point of view, the individual experience elements available at the touchpoints must first be (positively) perceive. Desired customer experiences can only occur when the customer becomes aware of the market services or experience elements and interacts with them. As such, apart from the customer solutions, implementation also means that *the marketing strategy (Sect. 5.3.2)* should also be *integrated and orchestrated*. The following integration strategies are possible (see IPA, 2011):

- *Advertising idea-oriented integration*: Communication across all media is based on a central creative central idea.
- *Brand-oriented integration:* Communication is based on a unified brand concept, which is often built on the organisation's core brand values.
- *Dialog-oriented integration*: The goal is to create a common dialog or conversation across all channels.

The effectiveness of these integration strategies depends on the intended objective. For customer acquisition, advertising-oriented integration is suitable, as it can, for example create new buying impulses. Brand-oriented integration is more suitable for retaining customers or preventing them from leaving, as it is based on long-term values and customer relationships. Dialog-oriented integration is particularly suitable for brand building and brand awareness, while it tends to pay less attention to short-term sales.

From the perspective of customer experience management, the primary focus should be on dialog-oriented and brand-oriented integration. Practical experience shows that advertising-oriented integration is less suitable in the context of customer experience-centred offerings due to its rather short-term and revenue-oriented nature. The short-term nature increases the risk that this form of integration will not adequately pick up on the corporate DNA designed for the long term.

In addition, just as a concert is orchestrated by many different stakeholders, it also takes the coordination and cooperation of different organisational units and processes to orchestrate the customer experiences. The Flywheel model explains the momentum an organisation gains when it is aligned around delivering strong customer experiences (Hubspot, 2021).

In order to increase the momentum of the flywheel, companies need to understand the importance of force and friction. To drive growth, organisations need to increase forces through the implementation of business strategies, e.g. marketing and communications, customer service and product development. As the wheel gains momentum due to the added force, organisations need to ensure that its efforts are not compromised by organisational friction. Friction can be a result of poor internal processes, culture, departments working in silos, poor customer service, unreasonable pricing, poor customer experience management and more. For instance, a marketing department and operations department have different goals, one to drive traffic and revenue and the other to reduce costs. If the departments only focus on their department goals, the flywheel will slow down due to the divergence of forces. Instead, organisations need to ensure that all units share the common goal of creating strong customer experience such that all operations and decisions are made on this basis and that the other goals are important but secondary. With all departments working towards the same goal of delivering remarkable customer experiences, the momentum of the flywheel can be continually sustained, leading to exponential growth.

6.2.2 Feedback Loop

Last but not least, one of the keys to maintaining strong customer experience is proactivity and reactivity. Every customer experience element implementation should be accompanied by a feedback mechanism to gather information from customers about their experience to enable companies to measure the effectiveness of the experience elements implemented. This could come in various forms, such as analytics tracking, surveys, and interviews. For example it is recommended that companies conduct regular quick surveys including questions that are related to the metrics in Sect. 2.3.3 after an interaction like a customer service call to evaluate that specific process. The information collected here can help companies assess if the specific touchpoint is performing up to expectations. In the case of undesired performances, the company is able to act in a timely manner to optimise the specific touchpoint. Furthermore, customers who had a poor experience can also be promptly handled through a personalised interaction with the aim to salvage the experience and prevent churn. In addition, as mentioned in Sect. 2.3.1, it is not only important to be able to understand the customer experience at each touchpoint but also the overall customer experience. As such, surveys should also come at the end of the customer journey (e.g. post-purchase and post-usage) to allow companies to evaluate the macro-experience.

As mentioned earlier, apart from the direct solicitation of feedback from customers, companies can also leverage on social media monitoring tools to understand what customers are saying about them and their experiences in their natural and private spheres. By being attentive to customer expressions about their experiences, companies can gain valuable insights about customer expectations, potential improvements, and even future offers.

References

Albert, W., & Tullis, T. (2013). *Measuring the user experience: Collecting, analyzing, and presenting usability metrics.* Elsevier Science & Technology. Accessed July 9, 2021, from ProQuest Ebook Central.

Björklund, C. (2019). *App maintenance cost can be three times higher than development cost.* Accessed September 26, 2021, from https://www.econnectivity.se/app-maintenance-cost-can-be-three-times-higher-than-development-cost/

IPA. (2011). Integration: How to get it right and deliver results. In: *Summary of an Institute of Practitioners in Advertising members report.*

Hubspot. (2021). *The flywheel.* Accessed August 1, 2021, from https://www.hubspot.com/flywheel

Stegemann, M., & Suwelack, T. (2020). A/B-testing – A method for optimizing the digital interaction of consumers and companies. In S. Boßow-Thies, C. Hofmann-Stölting, & H. Jochims (Eds.), *Data-driven marketing.* Springer Gabler.

Valuy, S. (2020). *How to build an MVP: The best feature prioritization techniques.* Accessed August 1, 2021, from https://dzone.com/articles/how-to-build-an-mvp-the-best-feature-prioritization

Wang, J. H., Antonenko, P., Celepkolu, M., Jimenez, Y., Fieldman, E., & Fieldman, A. (2019). Exploring relationships between eye tracking and traditional usability testing data. *International Journal of Human–Computer Interaction, 35*(6), 483–494. https://doi.org/10.1080/10447318.2018.1464776

Yoskovitz, B. (2011). *How to prioritize feature development after launching an MVP*. Accessed August 1, 2021, from https://www.instigatorblog.com/how-to-prioritize-feature-development-after-launching-an-mvp/2011/02/02/

7

Future Considerations

A customer experience-centric organisation can only be created if customer experience becomes the centre of the organisation. Strong customer experience must be the first drop of water that sends a ripple through all organisational decisions and actions. The customer experience framework in this book covers all the core areas and processes which need to be carefully managed in order to facilitate the ripple effect. Apart from what has been covered in the framework, there are also several other areas that companies can further explore to make their CEM process more robust.

CEM is not only the role of a single department but of the entire organisation. The orchestration of strong customer experiences across the customer journey requires a seamless cooperation of the various departments, from product development to marketing to information technology and human resources. It is crucial that the customer experience strategy of the company is strongly embedded in every department. Companies which place the responsibility of CEM on an individual department are unlikely to orchestrate a seamless macro-experience as the end customer experience could be inconsistent. Apart from the product development team who needs to understand customers and identify needs to generate new product and solution ideas, many processes have to happen after that to ensure that it is effectively implemented into the customer journey. For instance, the marketing team needs to design promotional, and pricing strategies oriented towards the target customer and align its marketing strategies. Service operations also need to ensure that customer processes are aligned with the desired customer experience and properly executed at every touchpoint. Next, the IT team also plays a crucial role, especially in the age of digitisation where offerings are increasingly available online on e-commerce sites. In the online world, user experience is key, and the IT team needs to ensure that the technical implementation supports the delivery of strong customer experiences and that user data is collected from all relevant touchpoints and stored. Lastly, the HR team is also responsible for the internal marketing of the importance of CX and to help employees understand how they can work together to effectively manage it, e.g. performance evaluation is not solely based on department goals but CX-related organisational goals and metrics (Meyer and Schwager, 2007). Very importantly, the entire organisation needs to come together to share their knowledge and cooperate to ensure effective CEM.

As briefly mentioned, in order for companies to consistently create strong customer experiences, they need to be able to measure the outcome of their CEM efforts and learn from statistics. This means that it is crucial that companies set up a data collection and storage system such as a CRM tool. The implementation of such a tool will support the analysis of data that can generate insights that are helpful in informing business decisions. In addition, a system like this can also help companies facilitate the sharing of customer information which ensures that various departments work with the same database for seamless management. For start-ups, it will take some time to see data in their systems, but it is certainly a good practice to have it set up right at the initial stages to prevent any data loss. From a long-term perspective, having a rich quantity of customer data can enable machine learning, which can help to support the CEM process by anticipating future customer needs.

To conclude, it is not only important to create strong customer experiences but to ensure that the orchestration effectively translates into desired perceptions. As such, the iterative process of CEM cannot be further emphasised. Apart from the content covered in this book, startups should also look into complementary topics such as project management, finance and funding, legal, HR and technology, which can support and complement the organisational strategy.

Reference

Meyer, C., & Schwager, A. (2007). Understanding customer experience. *Harvard Business Review.* https://idcexed.com/wp-content/uploads/2021/01/Understanding_Customer_Experience.pdf

Your Key Takeaways from the Book

Customer experience is not just a buzzword, and its significance cannot be undermined. While many companies see the value of making CX a focus, some struggle with getting started, and others fail to invest time and resources in truly managing it. Creating a customer experience-centric start-up requires putting the customer and customer experiences at the centre of all business decisions. It is not a one-time venture; it is a long-term endeavour that companies need to commit to on a continuous basis. The theoretical knowledge and practical tools provided in this toolbox provide an easy-to-follow process for practitioners to include in their daily management of the organisation for the successful development and implementation of their customer experience-centric business activities. With this framework, practitioners gain a clear and concrete "roadmap" to attract and retain customers and lead to an improvement of customer satisfaction, NPS and financial performance. Finally, readers will be able to better mentally locate and dive into the essential issues that matter in today's business world, which is the critical foundation for successfully implementing these in the organisation.

Appendix: Definitions of Customer Experience

Jain et al. (2017, pp. 649)	Customer experience is the aggregate of feelings, perceptions and attitudes formed during the entire process of decision-making and consumption chain involving an integrated series of interaction with people, objects, processes and environment, leading to cognitive, emotional, sensorial, and behavioural responses.
De Keyser et al. (2015, p. 23)	Defines customer experience as "comprised of the cognitive, emotional, physical, sensorial, spiritual, and social elements that mark the customer's direct or indirect interaction with (an) other market actor(s)"
Lemon and Verhoef (2016, p.71)	Customer experience is a multidimensional construct focusing on a customer's cognitive, emotional, behavioural, sensorial, and social responses to a firm's offerings during the customer's entire purchase journey.
Gartner (n.d.)	CX is the perception or the customer's conscious thoughts and feelings associated with it, which is/are evoked by the interaction(s) with a company's employees, channels, systems, and products.
Bordeaux (2021)	Customer experience is the impression your customers have of your brand as a whole throughout all aspects of the buyer's journey. It results in their view of your brand and impacts factors related to your bottom-line, including revenue.

References

Bordeaux, J. (2021). *What is customer experience? (and why it's so important)*. Accessed June 20, 2021, from https://blog.hubspot.com/service/what-is-customer-experience

De Keyser, A., Verleye, K., Lemon, K. N., Keiningham, T., & Klaus, P. (2015). *A framework for understanding and managing the CX*. Marketing Science Institute Working Paper Series 2015, Report No. 15-121. Marketing Science Institute.

Gartner. (n.d.). *Customer experience. Gartner Glossary*. Accessed June 15, 2021, from https://www.gartner.com/en/information-technology/glossary/customer-experience

Jain, R., Aagja, J., & Bagdare, S. (2017). Customer experience – a review and research agenda. *Journal of Service Theory and Practice, 27*(3), 642–662. https://doi.org/10.1108/JSTP-03-2015-0064

Lemon, K. N., & Verhoef, P. (2016). Understanding customer experience throughout the customer journey. *Journal of Marketing, 80*, 69–96.

GPSR Compliance

The European Union's (EU) General Product Safety Regulation (GPSR) is a set of rules that requires consumer products to be safe and our obligations to ensure this.

If you have any concerns about our products, you can contact us on

ProductSafety@springernature.com

In case Publisher is established outside the EU, the EU authorized representative is:

Springer Nature Customer Service Center GmbH
Europaplatz 3
69115 Heidelberg, Germany

www.ingramcontent.com/pod-product-compliance
Lightning Source LLC
LaVergne TN
LVHW040914270326
834689LV00079B/7